CAREERS FOR

BORN LEADERS

& Other Decisive Types

Careers for You Series

CAREERS FOR

BORN LEADERS

& Other Decisive Types

BLYTHE CAMENSON

SECOND EDITION

McGraw·Hill

New York   Chicago   San Francisco   Lisbon   London   Madrid   Mexico City
Milan   New Delhi   San Juan   Seoul   Singapore   Sydney   Toronto

The *McGraw·Hill* Companies

Library of Congress Cataloging-in-Publication Data

Camenson, Blythe
     Careers for born leaders & other decisive types / Blythe Camenson— 2nd ed.
         p.   cm. — (McGraw-Hill careers for you series)
         ISBN 0-07-143857-2 (alk. paper)
         1. Executives—Vocational guidance.   2. Career development.   3. Executive
ability.   4. Leadership.   I. Title: Careers for born leaders and other decisive
types.   II. Title.   III. Series.

   HD38.2.C358   2005
   658.4'0023'73—dc22   2004018872

1 2 3 4 5 6 7 8 9 0   DOC/DOC   0 9 8 7 6 5

ISBN 0-07-143857-2

McGraw-Hill books are available at special quantity discounts to use as premiums and
sales promotions, or for use in corporate training programs. For more information,
please write to the Director of Special Sales, Professional Publishing, McGraw-Hill,
Two Penn Plaza, New York, NY 10121-2298. Or contact your local bookstore.

This book is printed on acid-free paper.

Contents

. . . .

Acknowledgments

The author would like to thank the following born leaders for providing information about their careers:

Julie Benthal, Vice President, Nursing Administration
Diane Camerlo, In-House Counsel, Federal Reserve Bank
LeAnne Coury, Assistant Director of Sales
Laurie DeJong, Assistant Director, Physical Therapy
Linda Dickinson, Chef and Menu Planner
Chris Fuller, Senior Vice President General Management
Jonas Martin Frost, U.S. Representative
Larry Morin, Senior Vice President, Customer Relations
Laura Murray, School Superintendent
George Ragsdale, Vice President, Engineering
Missy Soleau, Food and Beverage Manager
Ernie Stetenfeld, Public Relations Director
Kevin Whelan, Marketing/Product Manager

The editors would like to thank Josephine Scanlon for preparing this second edition.

CHAPTER ONE

Examining the Options

You're a leader, not a follower; you're the driver, not a passenger. You want a position of leadership, and though you know reaching the top rung on the ladder might take years of work, you're willing to prepare yourself for that climb.

No matter the setting—financial institutions, the government, corporations, educational facilities, or scores of others—there are certain skills and qualifications you'll need to get to the top. *Careers for Born Leaders* gives you a close-up look at some leadership roles and tells you how to prepare for these careers.

What Makes a Born Leader?

Effective leaders, whether they are executives, administrators, managers, or involved in other supervisory roles, come from a variety of backgrounds. They bring different experiences and personalities to their positions, but they all share some similar attributes.

Highly developed personal skills are essential for anyone interested in becoming a general manager or top executive. An analytical mind and the ability to quickly assess large amounts of information and data are also very important. Add to the list the ability to evaluate the interrelationships of numerous factors and to select the best course of action. Sound intuitive judgment is crucial to reaching favorable decisions, often in the absence of sufficient hard information. General managers and top executives must also be able to communicate clearly and persuasively with customers, subordinates, and other managers in their firms. They must be confident, motivated, able to motivate others, decisive, and—probably most important—flexible.

Jobs for Born Leaders

General managers and top executives hold more than three million jobs in the United States. They are found in government and in every industry imaginable. Service-providing industries, including government, employ almost eight out of ten top-level executives.

Senators and representatives, chief executive officers, executive vice presidents for marketing, corporate in-house counsel, financial-institution vice presidents, department-store managers, brokerage-office managers, college deans, school superintendents, hospital administrators, and fire chiefs are examples of general managers and top executives who, at the upper end of the management hierarchy, formulate the policies and direct the operations of private firms and government agencies.

Many top executive positions are filled by promoting experienced, lower-level managers when an opening occurs. Some companies prefer that their top executives have specialized backgrounds—in finance or marketing, for example. In small firms, where the number of positions is limited, advancement to higher management positions may come slowly. In large firms, promotions may occur more quickly.

General managers may advance to top executive positions, such as executive or administrative vice president, in their own firms, or to corresponding general manager positions in larger firms. Similarly, top-level managers may advance to the peak corporate positions of chief operating officer and, finally, chief executive officer. Chief executive officers and other top executives may also become members of the board of directors of one or more firms. Some general managers and top executives with sufficient capital and experience establish their own firms or become independent consultants.

Executives and managers can increase their chances for advancement by participating in company training programs that impart broader knowledge of company policy and operations. Managers can also help advance their careers by becoming familiar with the latest developments in management techniques through national or local training programs sponsored by various industry and trade associations.

Managers who have experience in a particular field, such as accounting or engineering, may attend executive development programs in that field to facilitate their promotion to an even higher level. Participation in conferences and seminars can expand knowledge of national and international issues influencing the organization and can help participants network to develop useful contacts.

Born Leaders on the Job

The fundamental objective of private organizations is to maintain efficiency and profitability in the face of shifting consumer tastes and needs, accelerating technological complexity, economic interdependence, and domestic and foreign competition. Similarly, nonprofit organizations and government agencies must effectively implement programs that are subject to budgetary constraints and shifting public preferences. General managers and top executives in both public and private sectors work to ensure that their organizations meet their objectives.

An organization's general goals and policies are established by the chief executive officer in collaboration with other top executives, usually executive vice presidents, and often with a board of directors. In a large corporation, a chief executive officer meets frequently with subordinate executives to ensure that operations are conducted in accordance with these policies. Meetings may also occur with top executives of other corporations, domestic or foreign governments, or outside consultants to discuss matters affecting the organization's policies.

The chief executive officer of a corporation retains overall accountability; however, a chief operating officer may be delegated several responsibilities, including the authority to oversee executives who direct the activities of various departments and implement the organization's policies on a day-to-day basis. In publicly held and nonprofit corporations, the board of directors ultimately is accountable for the success or failure of the enterprise, and the chief executive officer reports to the board.

The nature of other high-level executives' responsibilities depends upon the size of the organization. In large organizations, the duties of such executives are highly specialized. Some managers, for instance, are responsible for the overall performance of one aspect of the organization, such as manufacturing, marketing, sales, purchasing, finance, personnel, training, administrative services, computer and information systems, property management, transportation, or legal services.

General managers direct their individual department's activities within the framework of the organization's overall plan. With the help of supervisory managers and their staffs, general managers oversee and strive to motivate workers to achieve their department's goals as rapidly and economically as possible. In smaller organizations, such as independent retail stores or small manufacturers, a general manager may be responsible for purchasing, hiring, training, quality control, and all other day-to-day supervisory duties.

Top executives typically have spacious offices and numerous support staff. General managers in large firms or nonprofit organizations usually have comfortable offices close to those of the top executives to whom they report. Long hours, including evenings and weekends, are standard for most top executives and general managers, although their schedules may be flexible.

Substantial travel is often required. General managers may travel between national, regional, and local offices to monitor operations and meet with customers, staff, and other executives. Top executives may travel to meet with their counterparts in other corporations in the country or overseas. Many attend meetings and conferences that are sponsored by industries and associations. The conferences provide an opportunity to meet with prospective donors, customers, contractors, or government officials and allow managers and executives to keep abreast of technological and managerial innovations. Perks such as reimbursement of an accompanying spouse's travel expenses may help executives cope with frequent or extended periods away from home.

In large organizations, job transfers between local offices or subsidiaries are common for employees on the executive career track. Top executives are under intense pressure to succeed; depending on the organization, this may mean earning higher profits, providing better service, or attaining fundraising and charitable goals. Executives in charge of poorly performing organizations or departments usually find their jobs in jeopardy.

Training for Born Leaders

The educational background of managers and top executives varies as widely as the nature of their diverse responsibilities. Many general managers and top executives have bachelor's degrees in liberal arts or business administration, and their majors often are related to the departments they direct. For example, a general manager of finance would likely have majored in accounting, while a general manager of information systems would commonly hold a degree in computer science. On the other hand, in some industries, such as retail trade, competent individuals without college degrees may become general managers.

Graduate and professional degrees are common in the ranks of top executives. Many managers in administrative, marketing, financial, and manufacturing activities have master's degrees in business administration. Managers in highly technical manufacturing and research activities often have master's or doctoral degrees in engineering or scientific disciplines.

Law degrees are mandatory for general managers of corporate legal departments, and hospital administrators generally have master's degrees in health services administration or business administration. College presidents generally have doctorates in the field in which they originally taught. School superintendents usually have doctorates, often in education administration.

Many general managers in the public sector have liberal arts degrees in public administration or in one of the social sciences, such as economics, psychology, sociology, or urban studies. For park superintendents, degrees in recreation and resource management provide suitable background. Police and fire chiefs are graduates of their respective academies, and degrees in police or fire science or related fields are increasingly important. For others, experience is still the primary qualification.

The Road Ahead

Employment of top executives and general managers is expected to grow about as fast as the average for all occupations through 2012. Because top managers are essential to the success of any organization, they should be more immune to automation and corporate restructuring—factors that are expected to adversely affect employment of lower-level managers.

Projected employment growth for top executive positions varies by industry, reflecting the projected change in industry employment over the 2002–12 period. For example, employment growth is expected to be faster than average in professional, scientific, and technical services as well as in administrative and support services. However, employment is projected to decline in some manufacturing industries.

Keen competition is expected for top executive positions, with the prestige and high pay attracting a large number of qualified applicants. Because this is a large occupation, numerous openings will occur each year as executives transfer to other positions, start their own businesses, or retire. However, many executives who leave their jobs transfer to other executive positions, which tends to limit the number of job openings for new entrants.

Managers whose accomplishments reflect strong leadership qualities and the ability to improve the efficiency or competitive positions of their organizations will have the best opportunities in all industries. In an increasingly global economy, certain types of experience, such as international economics, marketing, or information systems, or knowledge of several disciplines, will also be advantageous.

Top Salaries for Born Leaders

General managers and top executives are among the highest-paid workers in the nation. However, salary levels vary substantially depending upon the level of managerial responsibility and the length of service as well as the type, size, and location of the firm.

At the highest level, chief executive officers (CEOs) are extremely well paid. Median annual earnings of CEOs in 2002 were $126,260. Median annual earnings in the industries employing the largest numbers of chief executives in 2002 were as follows:

Management of companies and enterprises	$145,600
Architectural, engineering, and related services	$133,880
Banking and financial enterprises	$123,220
Colleges, universities, and professional schools	$103,120
Local government	$73,990

Salaries vary substantially by type and level of responsibility and by industry. According to a recent survey by Abbott, Langer &

Associates, the median income of chief executive officers in the nonprofit sector was $81,000 in 2003, but some of the highest paid made $600,000.

In addition to salaries, total compensation often includes stock options, dividends, and other performance bonuses. The use of executive dining rooms and company aircraft and cars, expense allowances, and company-paid insurance premiums and physical examinations also are among benefits commonly enjoyed by top executives in private industry. A number of chief executive officers are also provided with company-paid club memberships, chauffeured limousines, and other amenities.

Median annual earnings of general and operations managers in 2002 were $68,210. The middle 50 percent earned between $45,720 and $104,970. Because the specific responsibilities of general and operations managers vary significantly between industries, earnings also tend to vary considerably.

Median annual earnings in the industries that employed the largest numbers of general and operations managers in 2002 were as follows:

Management of companies and enterprises	$94,600
Building equipment contractors	$74,550
Banking and financial enterprises	$68,110
Local government	$60,470
Grocery stores	$44,980

CHAPTER TWO

Government Bigwigs

G o to school. Pay your taxes. Register for the draft. Stop at the stop sign. It seems as though the government is always telling us what to do. Who, then, tells the government what to do? Chief executives and legislators at the federal, state, and local levels do. They are elected or appointed officials who strive to meet the needs of their constituents by ensuring an effective and efficient government.

Chief Executives

Chief executives are officials who run governmental units that help formulate, carry out, and enforce laws. These officials include the president and vice president of the United States, state governors and lieutenant governors, county executives, town and township officials, mayors, and managers of cities, counties, towns, and townships. Most chief executives are elected by their constituents, but many managers are hired by a local government executive, council, or commission, to whom they are directly responsible. City, county, town, and other managers, although appointed officials, may act as, and refer to themselves as, chief executives.

Government chief executives, like their counterparts in the private sector, have overall accountability for the operations of their organizations. Working in conjunction with legislators, they establish goals for their constituencies and develop and coordinate the programs necessary to attain these goals. Government chief executives also appoint subordinates to head departments, such as highway, health, police, parks and recreation, finance, and economic development. These departments are staffed by civil servants who administer programs and enforce laws established by the legislative bodies. They also oversee budgets and ensure that resources are used properly and that programs are carried out as planned.

Chief executive officers manage a number of other important functions, such as meeting with legislators and constituents to determine the level of support needed for proposed programs. They confer with other government executives to solve mutual problems.

In addition, they often nominate citizens to boards and commissions to oversee government activities or to make recommendations for solving problems such as drug abuse, crime, deteriorating roads, and inadequate public education. They also solicit bids from and select contractors to do work for the government, encourage business investment and economic development in their jurisdictions, and seek federal or state funds to support various programs.

To accomplish all of these varied tasks effectively, chief executives of large governments rely on a staff of highly skilled aides to research issues that concern the public. Those in small local governments often do much of the work themselves.

Legislators

Legislators are elected officials who develop, enact, or amend laws. They include U.S. senators and representatives, state senators and representatives (called assemblymen and assemblywomen or delegates in some states), county legislators (called supervisors, commissioners, councilors, council members, or freeholders in some states), and city and town council members (called aldermen and alderwomen, trustees, clerks, supervisors, magistrates, and commissioners, among other titles).

Legislators introduce, examine, and vote on bills to pass official legislation. In preparing such legislation, they study staff reports and hear testimony from constituents, representatives of special-interest groups, board and commission members, and others with an interest in the issue under consideration. They usually must approve budgets and the appointments of nominees for leadership posts whose names are submitted by the chief executive. In some jurisdictions, the legislative council appoints the city, town, or county manager. Many legislators, especially at the state and federal levels, have a staff to help do research, prepare legislation, and resolve constituents' problems.

In some units of government, the line between legislative and executive functions blurs. For example, mayors and city managers may draft legislation and conduct council meetings, and council members may oversee the operation of departments.

Government Bigwigs on the Job

The working conditions of legislators and government chief executives vary with the size and budget of the governmental unit. Time spent at work ranges from a few hours a week for some local leaders to stressful weeks of sixty or more hours for members of the U.S. Congress. Some jobs require only occasional out-of-town travel, while others involve long periods away from home, such as when attending sessions of the legislature.

U.S. senators and representatives, governors and lieutenant governors, and chief executives in municipalities work full-time, year-round, as do most county and city managers. Many state legislators work full-time on government business while the legislature is in session (usually for two to six months a year or every other year) and work only part-time when the legislature is not in session. Some local elected officials work a schedule that is officially designated as part-time, but actually is the equivalent of a full-time schedule when unpaid duties are taken into account. In addition to their regular schedules, most chief executives are on call to handle emergencies.

Employment Figures

About five of six government chief executives and legislators work in local government; the rest work primarily in state governments. The federal government has 535 senators and representatives and two chief executives—the president and vice president. In 2002, sixty-seven thousand people were employed as legislators.

Chief executives and legislators who do not hold full-time, year-round positions normally work in a second occupation as well (commonly the one they held before being elected), are retired from another occupation, or attend to household responsibilities. Business owner or manager, teacher, and lawyer are common second occupations, and there are many others as well.

Training for Government Bigwigs

Apart from minimum age, residency, and citizenship requirements, candidates for legislative positions have no established training or qualifications criteria to meet. Legislative candidates come from a wide variety of occupations. Many have prior experience as lawyers, private-sector managers and executives, or business owners, and quite a few do have some political experience as staffers or members of government bureaus, boards, or commissions. Successful candidates usually become well known through their political campaigns, and some have built voter name recognition through their work with community, religious, fraternal, or social organizations.

Work experience and public service help develop the planning, organizing, negotiating, motivating, fund-raising, budgeting, public speaking, and problem-solving skills needed to run a political campaign. Candidates must make decisions quickly and fairly with little or contradictory information. They must have confidence in themselves and their employees to inspire and motivate their constituents and their staff. They should also be sincere and candid, presenting their views thoughtfully and convincingly.

Increasingly, candidates target information to voters through advertising paid for by their respective campaigns, so fund-raising skills are essential for prospective government executives. Additionally, they must know how to hammer out compromises with colleagues and constituents. National and statewide campaigns also require a good deal of energy and stamina.

A master's degree in public administration, including courses such as public financial management and legal issues in public administration, is widely recommended but not required. Virtually all town, city, and county managers have at least bachelor's degrees and many hold master's degrees.

In addition, working as a student intern in government is recommended. The experience and personal contacts acquired can prove invaluable in eventually securing a position as a town, city, or county manager.

Working in management support positions in government is an excellent way to gain the experience and personal contacts required to eventually secure a manager position. For example, applicants often have held jobs as management analysts or assistants in government departments, working for committees, councils, or chief executives.

In this capacity they learn about planning, budgeting, civil engineering, and other aspects of running a government. Generally, a town, city, or county manager is first hired by a smaller community, where he or she can gain expertise in the more complex financial and administrative matters needed to govern a larger jurisdiction.

Getting Ahead

Advancement opportunities for most elected public officials are not clearly defined. Because elected positions normally require a period of residency and because local public support is critical, officials can usually advance to other offices only in the jurisdictions where they live. For example, council members may run for mayor or for a position in the state government, and state legislators may run for governor or for Congress. Many officials are not politically ambitious, however, and do not seek advancement. Others lose their bids for reelection or voluntarily leave the occupation. A lifetime career as a government chief executive or legislator is rare.

Town, city, and county managers have a clearer career path: obtain a master's degree in public administration, then gain experience as a management analyst or as an assistant in a government department with a council and chief executive. After several years, such employees may be hired to manage towns or small cities and may eventually become managers of progressively larger cities.

The Road Ahead

Few new governments at any level are likely to be formed, and the number of chief executives and legislators in existing governments rarely changes. However, some increase will occur at the local level as counties, cities, and towns take on professional managers or move from volunteer to paid career executives to deal with population growth, federal regulations, and long-range planning.

Elections give newcomers the chance to unseat incumbents or to fill vacated positions. The level of competition in elections varies from place to place. There tends to be less competition in small communities that offer part-time positions with low or no salaries and little or no staff, compared with large municipalities with prestigious full-time positions offering high salaries, staff, and greater exposure.

Bigwigs, Big Bucks?

Salaries of public administrators vary widely, depending on the size of the government unit they serve and whether the job is full-time and year-round, part-time, or full-time for only a few months a year. Salaries range from little or nothing for a small-town council member to $400,000 a year for the president of the United States. In 2002, median annual earnings of legislators were $15,220, with the middle 50 percent earning between $13,180 and $38,540.

The National Conference of State Legislatures reports that the annual salary for rank-and-file legislators in the forty states that paid an annual salary ranged from $10,000 to more than $99,000 in 2003. In eight states, legislators received a daily salary plus an additional allowance for living expenses while legislatures were in session.

The Council of State Governments reports, in its *Book of the States, 2002–2003*, that gubernatorial salaries ranged from $50,000 a year in American Samoa to $179,000 a year in New York. In addition to salary, most governors receive benefits such as transportation and an official residence. Lieutenant governors average over $57,000 annually.

In 2003, U.S. senators and representatives earned $154,700; the Senate and House majority and minority leaders earned $171,900; and the vice president earned $198,600.

What It's Really Like

Meet Jonas Martin Frost, U.S. Representative

Democrat Jonas Martin Frost was elected to Congress in 1978 as a representative from Texas in the Dallas–Fort Worth area. He graduated from the University of Missouri in Columbia in 1964 with two degrees—a B.A. in history and a B.Jour. (journalism). He earned his J.D. degree from Georgetown University Law Center, Washington, D.C., in 1970. Prior to coming to Congress, he was a reporter for the Wilmington, Delaware, daily newspaper and the *Congressional Quarterly* in Washington. He then practiced law in Dallas. He was also vice president of the Dallas Democratic Forum.

He began his service in the U.S. House of Representatives in January of 1979 and has served continuously since that date.

How Congressman Frost Got Started. "During the time of my employment by *Congressional Quarterly*, where I covered the events in Congress, I became convinced that I could be a good representative, serving the interests of my home district in Dallas, Texas. The experience at *CQ* gave me the insight and contacts within the House of Representatives to achieve a good start once I was elected in 1978."

Prior to running for elected office, Congressman Frost's first job was as a staffer on the *Fort Worth Press*. The experience he gained there enabled him to secure a job with a daily newspaper. He later joined a television panel in Dallas, reporting on legal matters in the community. The program, called "Newsroom," was anchored by Jim Lehrer.

When Congressman Frost decided to run for office, he realized the importance of choosing a district in which he would feel comfortable. Since he was born in Fort Worth and knew the Dallas–Fort Worth area well, he felt confident of his understanding of the community's views.

The congressman describes his preparation for running: "I went about talking to various known community leaders, political activists, and media representatives . . . all of whom would know the political atmosphere of the community. I was running against an incumbent congressman, and there is always a group that opposes an incumbent, so it was a bit easier to create a political organization on that basis, rather than running in a district in which no incumbent was running.

"I chose the Democratic party because I believe the general philosophy of the party is closer to my own feelings on how people should be treated by the government, what role the government plays in daily lives, the extent to which government should develop, and so on. This is a very personal consideration that comes after years of watching the direction in which a particular party will lead the nation when that party is in power."

Congressman Frost explains that three important factors influenced his decision to run for the House of Representatives rather than the Senate. First, running for the Senate would require a level of familiarity and confidence with the entire state, rather than knowing one district well. Second, he was financially able to run a local campaign, whereas a statewide campaign would have been out of reach at the time. And third, experience gained as a reporter for the *Congressional Quarterly* taught him the rules and operations of the House of Representatives.

Congressman Frost describes the outcome of his first election: "I lost the first election in 1974. I was very disappointed, but I never had the slightest doubt that I would run again. I had received 46 percent of the vote in 1974, so it seemed that the goal was obtainable. After my loss in 1974, I practiced law until winning the election four years later, in 1978. . . . I have no plans to leave congressional service. If I were to retire or leave the service of the Congress for any reason, I would likely return to the practice of law in Dallas."

At the time of this writing, Congressman Frost is in his twelfth term in office. There are currently no term limits for serving in the House of Representatives, which has two-year terms of service. U.S. senators serve six-year terms.

Congressman Frost—On the Job. "My responsibilities now are to vote on issues that are important to my district and the nation as a whole. In the Congress, I represent over 566,000 people, and while it is difficult to represent all of them on the same issues, I must try to bring as many pertinent facts together to make a decision on issues in the best interest of these groups."

The congressman's day typically begins at 6:00 A.M. and lasts until about 10:00 P.M. The lighter items on his schedule include receptions and ceremonies, such as swearing-in ceremonies for new citizens or constituents who are named to public offices and dedications of new businesses. He also attends constituent meetings to inform his constituency about congressional matters.

The more difficult part of the job involves attending lengthy committee meetings. These meetings are important because they provide information on bills that could have wide-reaching effects, such as those mandating draft registration, income taxes, or environmental issues.

Congressman Frost is honest about the demands of his position. As he says, "The job can be very tiring, especially the many trips on airplanes that are required to return to my congressional district to make personal appearances to report on the activities of Congress and to meet with constituents about problems they are having—in an effort to help them if I can. There are always a variety of problems: sons or daughters wanting to get into military academies; companies unilaterally trying to eliminate health insurance programs for their retired employees; obtaining emergency loans for farmers who lose crops because of drought or flood—that sort of thing."

Fortunately, there is also an upside: "The work atmosphere is enjoyable. The Congress of the United States is generally composed of hardworking men and women who spend many hours in their efforts to make the United States a better nation. Washington, D.C., is our historic capital, and it is always a thrill and honor to be able to work here as I do.

"I like having the opportunity to have direct input into the decision-making function for our government. I represent more than 566,000 people on every issue that I vote on, and few people ever have that chance."

Advice from Congressman Frost. Congressman Frost offers some valuable advice for anyone considering a career in government service: "If you have a desire to serve in public office, you should be absolutely sure of your willingness to serve long hours and to take a lot of criticism for your decisions—because you cannot represent everyone's position on every issue.

"If you make the decision that you want to seek public office . . . then do so. It is a meaningful experience in just seeking the office, whether you win or lose. I lost the first race I made for Congress. Four years later, I still had the dream of serving in the Congress. I ran again and won."

CHAPTER THREE

Education Administrators

Every educational institution requires experienced and well-trained administrators to facilitate its smooth operation. Education administrators provide instructional leadership and manage the day-to-day activities in schools, colleges, universities, preschools, and day-care centers. They also direct the educational programs of businesses, correctional institutions, museums, and job-training and community-service organizations.

The Role of Education Administrators

Education administrators set educational standards and goals and establish the policies and procedures to carry them out. They also supervise managers, support staff, teachers, counselors, librarians, coaches, and other staff members. They develop academic programs, monitor students' educational progress, train and motivate teachers and other staff, and manage guidance and other student services.

These administrators also manage record keeping; prepare budgets; handle relations with parents, prospective and current students, employers, and the community; and perform many other duties. In an organization such as a small day-care center, one administrator may handle all these functions. In universities or large school systems, responsibilities are divided among many administrators, each with a specific function.

Elementary and Secondary School Administrators

Principals

Principals manage elementary, middle, and secondary schools. They set the academic tone for the institution, making high-quality instruction their main responsibility. Principals hire and evaluate teachers and other staff and help them to improve their skills. They confer with staff to advise, explain school programs and policies, and answer procedural questions.

Principals visit classrooms, observe teaching methods, review instructional objectives, and examine learning materials. They actively work with teachers to develop and maintain high curriculum standards, develop mission statements, and set performance goals and objectives.

Principals also meet and interact with other administrators, students, parents, school board members, and representatives of community organizations. Because decision-making authority has increasingly shifted from school district central offices to individual schools, parents, teachers, and other community members play an important role in setting school policies and goals. Principals must pay attention to the concerns of these groups when making administrative decisions.

These administrators prepare budgets and reports on various subjects, including finances and attendance, and they oversee the requisition and allocation of supplies. As school budgets become tighter, many principals have become more involved in public relations and fund-raising to secure financial support for their schools from local businesses and the community.

Principals must take an active role to ensure that students meet national, state, and local academic standards. Many develop partnerships with local businesses and school-to-work transition programs for students. Increasingly, principals must be sensitive to the needs of the rising number of non-English-speaking and

culturally diverse students. Growing enrollments, which are leading to overcrowding at many existing schools, also are a cause for
concern. When addressing problems of inadequate resources,
administrators serve as advocates for the building of new schools
or the repair of existing ones. During summer months, principals
are responsible for planning for the upcoming year, overseeing
summer school, participating in workshops for teachers and
administrators, supervising building repairs and improvements,
and working to be sure the school has adequate staff for the school
year.

Schools continue to be involved with students' emotional wel-
fare as well as their academic achievement. As a result, principals
face responsibilities outside the academic realm. For example, in
response to the growing numbers of dual-income and single-
parent families and teenage parents, schools have established
before- and after-school child-care programs or family resource
centers, which also may offer parenting classes and social service
referrals. With the help of community organizations, some principals have established programs to combat increases in crime,
drug and alcohol abuse, and sexually transmitted diseases among
students.

Assistant Principals

Assistant principals aid the principal in the overall administration
of the school. They are primarily responsible for scheduling student classes, ordering textbooks and supplies, and coordinating
transportation, custodial, cafeteria, and other support services.
They usually handle student discipline and attendance problems,
social and recreational programs, and health and safety matters.
They also may counsel students on personal, educational, or vocational matters.

With the increasing shift of management from the central districts to individual schools, assistant principals are playing a greater
role in ensuring the academic success of students by helping to
develop new curriculums, evaluating teachers, and dealing with

school-community relations—responsibilities previously assumed solely by the principal. The number of assistant principals that a school employs may vary, depending on the number of students.

Other Administrators

Superintendents. These administrators oversee entire school districts, interacting with the school board and with principals and administrators at all elementary, middle, and secondary schools within the district. They are the top administrators responsible for hiring school principals, monitoring overall effectiveness of schools, planning district-wide budgets, and preparing requests for school funding.

Central-Office Administrators. These executives operate within school district central offices. They include those who direct subject-area programs such as language arts, music, vocational education, special education, and mathematics. They plan, evaluate, and improve curriculums and teaching techniques and help teachers improve their skills and learn about new methods and materials. They oversee career counseling programs and testing that measures students' abilities and helps place them in appropriate classes.

Central-office administrators also include directors of programs such as guidance, school psychology, athletics, curriculum and instruction, and professional development. With the trend toward site-based management, principals and assistant principals, along with teachers and other staff, have primary responsibility for many of these programs in their individual schools.

College and University Administrators

Deans

In colleges and universities, academic deans assist the president. They make faculty appointments, develop budgets, and establish academic policies and programs. Often referred to as deans of faculty, provosts, or university deans, they direct and coordinate the activities of the individual colleges and the chairpersons of academic departments. Fund-raising is also becoming an essential part of the job.

Department Heads

College or university department heads or chairpersons are in charge of departments that specialize in particular fields of study, such as English, biological science, or mathematics. In addition to teaching, they coordinate schedules of classes and teaching assignments; recruit, interview, and hire applicants for teaching positions; evaluate faculty members; and encourage faculty development. They also propose budgets, serve on committees, and perform other administrative duties. In overseeing their departments, chairpersons must consider and balance the concerns of faculty, administrators, and students.

Other Higher Education Administrators

Vice Presidents of Student Affairs. Often referred to as vice presidents of student life, deans of students, or directors of student services, these administrators may direct and coordinate admissions, foreign student services, health and counseling services, career services, financial aid, and housing and residential life. They also oversee a school's social, recreational, and related programs. In small colleges, they may counsel students. In larger colleges and universities, separate administrators may handle each of these services.

Registrars. These executives are custodians of students' records. They register students, record grades, prepare student transcripts, evaluate academic records, assess and collect tuition and fees, plan and implement commencement, oversee the preparation of college catalogs and schedules of classes, and analyze enrollment and demographic statistics.

Directors of Admissions. These directors manage the process of recruiting, evaluating, and admitting students and work closely with financial-aid directors, who oversee scholarship, fellowship, and loan programs.

Athletic Directors. Responsibilities of these directors include planning and directing intramural and intercollegiate athletic activities, overseeing publicity for athletic events, preparing budgets, and supervising coaches.

Other increasingly important administrators direct college fund-raising, public relations, distance learning, and technology.

Education Administrators on the Job

Education administrators hold leadership positions with significant responsibility. Most find working with students extremely rewarding, but as the responsibilities of administrators have increased in recent years, so has the stress. Coordinating staff and interacting with faculty, parents, students, and community members can be fast paced and stimulating but also stressful and demanding. Principals and assistant principals, whose varied duties include discipline, may find working with difficult students challenging.

Many education administrators work more than forty hours a week, often including school activities at night and on weekends. Most administrators work eleven or twelve months out of the year. Some jobs include travel.

Employment Figures

Education administrators held about 427,000 jobs in 2002. About two in ten worked for private education institutions, and six in ten worked for state and local governments, mainly in schools, colleges and universities, and departments of education. Less than 5 percent were self-employed. The rest worked in day-care centers, religious organizations, job-training centers, and businesses and other organizations that provide training for their employees.

Training for Education Administrators

Education administration is not usually an entry-level job. Most education administrators begin their careers in related occupations and prepare for a job in education administration by completing a master's or doctoral degree. Because of the diversity of duties and levels of responsibility, their educational backgrounds and experience vary considerably.

Principals, assistant principals, central-office administrators, academic deans, and preschool directors usually have held teaching positions before moving into administration. Some teachers move directly into principal positions; others first become assistant principals or gain experience in other central-office administrative jobs at either the school or district level in positions such as department head, curriculum specialist, or subject-matter advisor. In some cases, administrators move up from related staff jobs such as recruiter, guidance counselor, librarian, residence-hall director, or financial aid or admissions counselor.

Getting Ahead

To be considered for education administrator positions, workers must first prove themselves in their current jobs. In evaluating candidates, supervisors look for leadership, determination, confidence, innovativeness, and motivation. The ability to make sound decisions and to organize and coordinate work efficiently is essential.

A large part of an administrator's job involves interacting with others—such as students, parents, teachers, and the community—

so a person in such a position must have strong interpersonal skills and be an effective communicator and motivator. Knowledge of leadership principles and practices, gained through work experience and formal education, is important. Familiarity with the latest computer technology is also a necessity for principals, who are required to gather information and coordinate technical resources for their students, teachers, and classrooms.

In most public schools, principals, assistant principals, and school administrators in central offices need a master's degree in education administration or educational supervision. Some principals and central-office administrators have a doctorate or specialized degree in education administration. In private schools, which are not subject to state licensure requirements, some principals and assistant principals hold only a bachelor's degree; however, the majority have a master's or doctoral degree.

Most states require principals to be licensed as school administrators; license requirements vary by state. National standards for school leaders, including principals and supervisors, have been developed by the Interstate School Leaders Licensure Consortium under the guidance of the Council of Chief State School Officers. Many states use these national standards as guidelines to assess beginning principals for licensure. Increasingly, on-the-job training, often with a mentor, is required for new school leaders. Some states require administrators to take continuing education courses to maintain licensure, thus ensuring that administrators have the most up-to-date skills. The number and types of courses required to maintain licensure vary by state.

Academic deans and chairpersons usually have a doctorate in their specialty. Most have held a professorship in the department before advancing. Admissions, student affairs, and financial aid directors and registrars sometimes start in related staff jobs with bachelor's degrees—any field usually is acceptable—and obtain advanced degrees in college student affairs, counseling, or higher education administration. A Ph.D. or Ed.D. usually is necessary for top student affairs positions. Computer literacy and a background in accounting or statistics may be assets in admissions, records, and financial work.

Advanced degrees in higher education administration, educational supervision, and college student affairs are offered at many colleges and universities. The National Council for Accreditation of Teacher Education and the Educational Leadership Constituent Council accredit these programs, which include courses in school leadership, school law, school finance and budgeting, curriculum development and evaluation, research design and data analysis, community relations, politics in education, and counseling. Educational supervision degree programs include courses in supervision of instruction and curriculum, human relations, curriculum development, research, and advanced teaching courses.

Education administrators advance to more responsible administrative positions through promotion or by transferring to more responsible positions at larger schools or systems. They also may become superintendents of school systems or presidents of educational institutions.

The Road Ahead

Employment of education administrators is projected to grow faster than the average for all occupations through 2012. As education and training take on greater importance in everyone's lives, the need for people to administer education programs will grow. Job opportunities for many of these positions should also be excellent because a large proportion of education administrators are expected to retire over the next ten years.

A significant portion of job growth will stem from growth in the private and for-profit segments of education. Many of these schools cater to working adults, many of whom might not ordinarily participate in postsecondary education. These schools allow students to earn a degree, receive job-specific training, or update their skills in a convenient manner, such as through part-time programs or distance learning. As the number of these schools continues to grow, more administrators will be needed to oversee them.

Enrollment of school-age children will also have an impact on the demand for education administrators. The U.S. Department of Education projects enrollment of elementary and secondary school students to grow between 5 and 7 percent over the next decade. Administrators in preschools and child-care centers are expected to experience substantially more employment growth as enrollments in formal child-care programs continue to expand as fewer private households care for young children. Additionally, if mandatory preschool becomes more widespread, more preschool directors will be needed.

The number of postsecondary school students is projected to grow more rapidly than other student populations, creating significant demand for administrators at that level. In addition, enrollment is expected to increase the fastest in the West and South, where the population is growing, and to decline or remain stable in the Northeast and the Midwest. School administrators also are in greater demand in rural and urban areas, where pay is generally lower than in the suburbs.

Principals and assistant principals should have favorable job prospects. As principals are held more accountable for the performance of students and teachers, while at the same time required to adhere to a growing number of government regulations, fewer teachers have chosen to seek positions in administration. In addition, overcrowded classrooms, safety issues, budgetary concerns, and teacher shortages in some areas all are creating additional stress for administrators. For candidates who are not put off by these challenges, job opportunities should be plentiful.

Job prospects also are expected to be favorable for college and university administrators, particularly those seeking nonacademic positions. Colleges and universities may be subject to funding shortfalls during economic downturns, but increasing enrollment over the projection period will require that institutions replace the large numbers of administrators who retire as well as hire additional administrators.

While competition among faculty for prestigious positions as academic deans and department heads is likely to remain keen, fewer applicants are expected for nonacademic administrative jobs, such as director of admissions or student affairs. Furthermore, many people are discouraged from seeking administrator jobs by the requirement that they have a master's or doctoral degree in education administration. For those with the right qualifications, this should be a promising field.

Earnings for Education Administrators

Salaries of education administrators vary according to position, level of responsibility and experience, and the size and location of the institution. According to the Educational Research Service, average salaries for principals and assistant principals in the 2002–03 school year were as follows:

PRINCIPALS

Elementary school	$75,291
Junior high/middle school	$80,708
Senior high school	$86,452

ASSISTANT PRINCIPALS

Elementary school	$62,230
Junior high/middle school	$67,228
Senior high school	$70,874

According to the College and University Professional Association for Human Resources, median annual salaries for selected administrators in higher education in 2001–02 were as follows:

ACADEMIC DEANS

Arts and sciences	$98,780
Business	$107,414
Continuing education	$84,457
Education	$100,227
Graduate programs	$100,391
Health-related professions	$89,234
Nursing	$88,386
Occupational/vocational education	$73,595

STUDENT-SERVICES DIRECTORS

Admissions and registrar	$61,519
Dean of students	$70,012
Financial aid	$57,036
Student activities	$41,050

What It's Really Like

Meet Laura Murray, School Superintendent

Laura Murray is school superintendent with the Homewood-Flossmoor Community High School District 233 in Flossmoor, Illinois. Her school district has won the U.S. Department of Education Blue Ribbon Award for Educational Excellence and a national technology award. Her office is located in one of the district's school buildings.

Dr. Murray earned her bachelor's degree in mathematics from Purdue University in West Lafayette, Indiana, in 1972; her master's in secondary education in 1976 from Northern Illinois University in DeKalb; and her doctorate in educational leadership and policy studies in 1989 from Loyola University in Chicago. She also has a guidance and counseling certificate and has attended numerous professional conferences. She's been in education since 1972.

How Laura Murray Got Started. Laura graduated from high school in 1968. Her choice of a college major was directly influenced by some outstanding high school teachers, in particular Mr. Brown, a mathematics teacher. By the time Laura graduated from college, the district was constructing a new high school, Glenbard South. She interviewed for and won a position as a full-time math teacher at the new school. To Laura's delight, she ended up working with Mr. Brown, her former teacher.

Laura describes what happened first at her new job: "On the first day of teaching, they asked us all what we wanted to do in twenty years. I said, 'Be a high school principal.' That occurred nineteen years later. In between, here is what happened: After I taught for several years, coached tennis, coached the Pom Poms, and sponsored Student Council, the principal came to me and said, 'A guidance counselor is pregnant. Get your certificate and the job is yours.' I did. For two years I was a guidance counselor."

Laura quit her job in 1980 to stay at home with her infant son. Two months later, she found herself bored and missing work, so she called her former principal to ask if there were any jobs available. Laura was offered the position of dean of students. She took the job and stayed with it for two years. This was primarily a disciplinary role, and Laura had to deal with plenty of challenging situations. As she describes it, "During that time I got knocked in the jaw, skunked by a skunk, and had to pick up 1,981 mice that the seniors let go in the cafeteria as a graduation prank."

In June 1982 Laura was asked to take the position of director of guidance at a high school in a different district. She accepted the job because it seemed like a welcome change from discipline and offered a challenge.

Laura describes what she learned in this new job: "I revamped an entire department and learned that Machiavelli is right. As a leader, you have to learn to be respected—but maybe not liked or loved. That is a hard pill to swallow if you are a people person.

After three years in the job and a successful reorganization, I was called by my previous district and asked to come back as assistant principal. My current district did not want to lose me, so they made me the same offer.

"At that time I realized that, to be a high school principal, I would need a Ph.D., so I worked full-time on it while still being a mother, wife, and full-time assistant principal. When it was time to apply to be a principal, I realized it would be the first job I sought since applying as a math teacher. All the others had been offered to me."

Laura applied at Homewood-Flossmoor High School and was hired as principal. She worked for one year with the superintendent before he retired. The new superintendent only lasted a little over a year; when he left in 1993, Laura was named acting superintendent and principal. After several months the board of directors offered her the position of superintendent.

The decision to accept the position was not an easy one. As Laura says, "I had to really think about that because all I ever wanted to be was principal. After much soul-searching and networking with many friends, I decided to say yes. The key here is that I was going from a building-level position to a district position and didn't have any district experience. It was a first, but I am a quick study.

"Part of it was being in the right place at the right time. In Illinois there are only three superintendents of high school districts who are female. I was the second one.

"I entered education because I like students and I believe in public education. I am a real people-oriented person. I had role models in high school whom I really admired, so I chose this profession. The different jobs I had all came about because someone above me thought I would be good at the job and convinced me to try it."

Laura Murray—On the Job. "Officially, the superintendent of schools serves as the chief school officer of the Board of Education. I am responsible for the overall administration and supervision of the educational system and for all personnel and factors that directly or indirectly serve to direct and control the system."

Laura's primary functions include maintaining a relationship with the Board of Education, Instruction, and Curriculum; managing personnel (recommending, hiring, and evaluating); and handling fiscal affairs, management and operations, and community relations.

As Laura says, "The job is very busy, and I have to be able to juggle twenty things at once. It is very stressful and requires long hours. Days of twelve and fourteen hours are very typical, with many evening and weekend responsibilities.

"I spend much time on the telephone, meeting with people, and being a public relations person. I have learned to be an expert in conflict management and have spoken at many conferences on this topic."

Laura's day does not revolve around a set schedule. On any given day she might take several telephone calls and attend meetings with teachers and conferences with students and parents. She might also attend community meetings and visit classrooms. In addition to these duties, there is always the possibility of a crisis, such as a student fight involving a weapon, or an unanticipated special event. For example, Laura was once given four days' notice that President Bill Clinton would visit her school.

Laura describes the ups and downs of her work: "I love working with students and watching them grow and develop in four years of high school. It is gratifying to be in a position to effect change that will increase student learning, student self-esteem, and student motivation. I like the way no day is typical. I can be proactive, but I have learned how to be reactive in a positive way. I love to be busy and to do several activities at once. I like challenges, and this job is always a challenge or offers a puzzle to solve.

"What I like least is the stress, and sometimes dealing with negative people can be depressing. Also, one of the most important jobs of a superintendent is working with Board of Education members. I have a great board with whom I work, but I imagine it would be quite difficult and no fun working with board members who constantly disagreed with you and among themselves."

Advice from Laura Murray. Dr. Murray has some advice for anyone interested in pursuing a career in education administration: "First, do as many different jobs in the education setting as you can so you can see things from many viewpoints. Second, learn how to make decisions, deal with conflict, and plan strategically. Third, have outlets in your life that release stress and learn how to make time for yourself.

"This job also takes a very supportive family who likes to attend high school events."

CHAPTER FOUR

Financial Managers

lmost every firm, government agency, and organization has one or more financial managers. These professionals work as controllers, treasurers or finance officers, credit managers, cash managers, and risk and insurance managers. They oversee the preparation of financial reports, direct investment activities, and implement cash management strategies. As computers are increasingly used to record and organize data, many financial managers are spending more time developing strategies and implementing the long-term goals of their organizations.

In small firms, chief financial officers usually handle all financial management functions. However, in large firms, these officers oversee all financial management departments and help top managers develop financial and economic policy and establish procedures, delegate authority, and oversee the implementation of these policies. Highly trained and experienced financial managers head each financial department.

Options in Financial Management

Controllers

Controllers direct the preparation of financial reports that summarize and forecast the organization's financial position, such as income statements, balance sheets, and analyses of future earnings or expenses. Controllers also are in charge of preparing special reports required by regulatory authorities. Often, controllers oversee the accounting, audit, and budget departments.

Treasurers and Finance Officers

Treasurers and finance officers direct an organization's financial goals, objectives, and budgets. They oversee the investment of funds and manage associated risks, supervise cash management activities, execute capital-raising strategies to support a firm's expansion, and deal with mergers and acquisitions.

Credit Managers

Credit managers oversee the firm's issuance of credit. They establish credit-rating criteria, determine credit ceilings, and monitor the collections of past-due accounts. Managers specializing in international finance develop financial and accounting systems for the banking transactions of multinational organizations.

Cash Managers

Cash managers monitor and control the flow of cash receipts and disbursements to meet the business and investment needs of the firm. For example, cash-flow projections are needed to determine whether loans must be obtained to meet cash requirements or whether surplus cash should be invested in interest-bearing instruments.

Risk and Insurance Managers

Risk and insurance managers oversee programs to minimize risks and losses that might arise from financial transactions and business operations undertaken by the institution. They also manage the organization's insurance budget.

Other Positions in Financial Management

Financial institutions such as commercial banks, savings and loan associations, credit unions, and mortgage and finance companies employ other financial managers in addition to those mentioned above. These managers oversee various functions, such as lending, trusts, mortgages, and investments, or programs that might include sales, operations, or electronic financial services. They may be required to solicit business, authorize loans, and direct the investment of funds, always adhering to federal and state laws and regulations.

Branch managers of financial institutions administer and manage all of the functions of a branch office, which may include hiring personnel, approving loans and lines of credit, establishing a rapport with the community to attract business, and assisting customers with account problems. Financial managers who work for financial institutions must keep abreast of the rapidly growing array of financial services and products.

In addition to these general duties, all financial managers perform tasks unique to the specific organization or industry. For example, government financial managers must be experts on government appropriations and budgeting processes, whereas health-care financial managers must be knowledgeable about issues surrounding health-care financing. Moreover, financial managers must be aware of special tax laws and regulations that affect the industry.

Financial Managers on the Job

Financial managers work in comfortable offices, often close to top managers and to departments that develop the financial data that managers need. They typically have direct access to state-of-the-art computer systems and information services. Financial managers commonly work long hours, often up to fifty or sixty per week. They generally are required to attend meetings of financial and economic associations, and they may travel to visit subsidiary firms or to meet customers.

Employment Figures

Financial managers held about 599,000 jobs in 2002. While the vast majority of financial managers are employed in private industry, nearly one in ten works for the different branches of government. In addition, although they can be found in every industry, approximately one out of four are employed by insurance and finance establishments, such as banks, savings institutions, finance companies, credit unions, and securities dealers.

Training for Financial Managers

A bachelor's degree in finance, accounting, economics, or business administration is the minimum academic preparation for financial managers. However, many employers now seek graduates with master's degrees, preferably in business administration, economics, finance, or risk management. These academic programs help develop analytical skills and provide knowledge of the latest financial analysis methods and technology.

In some situations, experience may be more important than formal education for certain financial manager positions, particularly branch managers in banks. Banks typically fill branch manager positions by promoting experienced loan officers and other professionals who excel at their jobs. Other financial managers may enter the profession through formal management training programs offered by the company.

Continuing education is vital for financial managers, who must cope with the growing complexity of global trade, changes in federal and state laws and regulations, and the proliferation of new and complex financial instruments. Firms often provide opportunities for workers to broaden their knowledge and skills by encouraging employees to take graduate courses at colleges and universities or to attend conferences related to their specialties. Financial management, banking, and credit union associations, often in cooperation with colleges and universities, sponsor numerous national and local training programs. Those enrolled in such programs prepare extensively at home and then attend sessions on subjects such as accounting management, budget management, corporate cash management, financial analysis, international banking, and information systems. Many firms pay all or part of the costs for employees who successfully complete courses. Although experience, ability, and leadership are emphasized for promotion, advancement may be accelerated by this type of special study.

In some cases, financial managers also may broaden their skills and establish their competency by attaining professional certification. There are many different associations that offer professional certification programs. For example, the Association for Investment Management and Research confers the Chartered Financial Analyst designation on investment professionals who have a bachelor's degree, pass three sequential examinations, and meet work experience requirements. The Association for Financial Professionals confers the Certified Cash Manager credential to those who pass a computer-based exam and have a minimum of two years of relevant experience. The Institute of Management Accountants offers a Certified in Financial Management designation to members with a bachelor's degree and at least two years of work experience who pass the institute's four-part examination and fulfill continuing education requirements. Also, financial managers who specialize in accounting may earn the Certified Public Accountant (CPA) or Certified Management Accountant (CMA) designations.

The Qualities You'll Need

Candidates for financial management positions need a broad range of skills. Interpersonal skills are important because these jobs involve managing people and working as part of a team to solve problems. Financial managers must have excellent communication skills to explain complex financial data. Because financial managers work extensively with various departments in the firm, a broad overview of the business is essential.

Financial managers should be creative thinkers and problem solvers, applying their analytical skills to business. They must be comfortable with the latest computer technology. As financial operations increasingly are affected by the global economy, financial managers must have knowledge of international finance. Proficiency in a foreign language also may be important in some positions.

Getting Ahead

Because financial management is critical for efficient business operations, well-trained, experienced financial managers who display a strong grasp of the operations of various departments within an organization are prime candidates for promotion to top management positions. Some financial managers transfer to closely related positions in other industries. Those with extensive experience and access to sufficient capital may start their own consulting firms.

The Road Ahead

Employment of financial managers is expected to grow about as fast as the average for all occupations through 2012. Growth is expected to be steady and will increase in line with the growth of the economy as a whole. However, job seekers are likely to face keen competition for jobs, as the number of job openings is expected to be less than the number of applicants. Candidates with expertise in accounting and finance, particularly those with a master's degree, should enjoy the best job prospects.

As the economy expands, job growth for financial managers will stem from both the expansion of established companies and from the creation of new businesses. In the short term, employment in this occupation is negatively affected by economic downturns, during which companies are more likely to close departments or even go out of business, thus decreasing the need for financial managers. Mergers, acquisitions, and corporate downsizing also are likely to adversely affect the employment of financial managers. Still, the growing need for financial expertise as the economy expands will ensure job growth over the next decade.

The banking industry, which employs more than one out of ten financial managers, will continue to consolidate, although at a slower rate than in previous years. In spite of this trend, employment of bank branch managers is expected to increase as banks begin to refocus on the importance of their existing branches and as new branches are created to serve a growing population. As banks expand the range of products and services they offer to include insurance and investment products, branch managers with knowledge in these areas will be needed. As a result, candidates who are licensed to sell insurance or securities will have the most favorable prospects.

Despite the current downturn in the securities and commodities industry, the long-run prospects for financial managers in that industry should be favorable, as more will be needed to handle increasingly complex financial transactions and manage a growing amount of investments. Financial managers also will be needed to handle mergers and acquisitions, raise capital, and assess global financial transactions. Risk managers, who assess risks for insurance and investment purposes, also will be in demand.

Some companies may hire financial managers on a temporary basis to see the organization through a short-term crisis or to offer suggestions for boosting profits. Other companies may contract out all accounting and financial operations. Even in these cases, however, financial managers will likely be needed to oversee the contracts.

Computer technology has reduced the time and staff required to produce financial reports. As a result, forecasting earnings, profits, and costs and generating ideas and creative ways to increase corporate profitability will become the major role of financial managers over the next decade. Financial managers who are familiar with computer software that can assist them in this role will be needed.

. . . .

Salaries for Financial Managers

Median annual earnings of financial managers were $73,340 in 2002. The middle 50 percent earned between $52,490 and $100,660. The lowest 10 percent had earnings of less than $39,120, while the top 10 percent earned over $142,260. Median annual earnings in the industries employing the largest numbers of financial managers in 2002 were as follows:

Securities and commodity contracts intermediation and brokerage	$125,220
Management of companies and enterprises	$88,310
Nondepository credit intermediation	$78,400
Local government	$63,090
Depository credit intermediation	$58,790

According to a 2002 survey by Robert Half International, a staffing services firm specializing in accounting and finance professionals, directors of finance earned between $75,000 and $204,500, and corporate controllers earned between $54,000 and $138,750.

The Association for Financial Professionals' annual compensation survey showed that financial officers' average total compensation in 2002, including bonuses and deferred compensation, was $130,900. Selected financial manager positions had average total compensation as follows:

Vice president of finance	$183,500
Treasurer	$150,600
Assistant vice president of finance	$141,300
Controller/comptroller	$134,300
Director	$113,600
Assistant treasurer	$111,900

Assistant controller/comptroller	$115,500
Manager	$84,500
Cash manager	$64,700

Large organizations often pay more than small ones, and salary levels also can depend on the type of industry and location. Many financial managers in both public and private industry receive additional compensation in the form of bonuses, which also vary substantially by size of firm. Deferred compensation in the form of stock options is becoming more common, especially for senior-level executives.

······························

What It's Really Like

Meet Larry Morin, Senior Vice President, Customer Relations

Larry Morin works as the head of customer relations for Fidelity Investments, National Financial Security Corporation, in New York City. He began working in the financial field in 1971 and has ten years of regional banking experience in Connecticut and Minnesota and twenty years in brokerage with Merrill Lynch, Shearson Lehman, and Fidelity Investments.

How Larry Morin Got Started. "It was serendipity. Most people I know did not set out to get the job they have on Wall Street. My neighbor was the head teller of Connecticut Bank and Trust. I needed a part-time job, and the bank was starting a new department called clearance.

"For every buy or sell of stocks and bonds, there is a corresponding delivery from the seller to the buyer. Each brokerage firm has an operating area that supports the settlement, or clearance, of these transactions. There are bookkeeping entries that reflect the transaction on each customer account. Say you buy a hundred shares of IBM. You buy them from your stockbroker.

Your broker, in turn, buys them from a broker for IBM. There are actual pieces of paper that cross hands from IBM to your broker- age company. They are 'delivered' and 'cleared' into your account. You also get copies. This is clearance. Stocks and bonds, in this case, are called securities."

Larry worked in clearance for five years. He became a full-time employee and learned all of the department's functions. Initially, he delivered securities to different banks. Once he learned more about the workings of securities, he says, "I got hooked. And in many ways, it is just like learning a whole new language."

Each security product has its own set of settlement and clear- ance activities, and Larry learned all about them. Government securities, government bonds, national securities, and bonds between nations are a few of the different types of items that Larry became familiar with. He also learned about the operations, or different departments, that handle transactions of stocks and bonds.

Larry took to the work and felt comfortable with what he was learning. As he says, "I learned that language quickly and looked for shortcuts and precision. I always asked what I could do and if anyone needed help."

When the head teller moved to a Minnesota company called Investors Diversified Service, a major mutual fund and investor advisory firm, Larry went with him to establish a clearance department. He was later introduced to someone from Merrill Lynch, and again he learned a new language and system. Once more, Larry was hooked.

"While moving up the corporate ladder from manager to senior vice president, I learned many aspects of the brokerage field. In Merrill, I learned operations. In Shearson, I ran operations and 'the cage,' which is the vault. Now, I'm running customer service."

Larry Morin—On the Job. As senior vice president of customer relations, Larry manages a staff of between one hundred and five hundred, with five to eight staff members reporting directly to him. He oversees the day-to-day functions of the department, such as customer service, tax reporting, transfer of accounts between firms, retirement account processing, opening new accounts, gain and loss reporting, and mail operations.

In addition to the daily responsibilities, Larry describes some of his other duties: "I also look at management reports and seek new ways of improving processing and service. In meetings with the people who report directly to me, I challenge them on numbers, trends, and performance, targeting improvement opportunities and trying to initiate people's thinking about the day-to-day and 'what ifs' (out-of-box thinking). I do this by asking questions about how to improve processing and by reducing rejects or things that have to be reprocessed because of mistakes. I initiate questions in our staff meetings that help the staff look at a problem in new ways in order to solve it. One of these ways is through brainstorming, where everyone throws out suggestions and we build from everyone's input."

Larry's typical work week is between forty-five and fifty hours. Each day is different, depending on the status of meetings and reports. On any given day, Larry might find himself working on an unanticipated problem, even though he was scheduled to attend a meeting on a different issue.

Larry describes some of the positive aspects of his job: "When you arrive at a breakthrough idea and see it implemented is the upside to this job. People then embrace the vision (the project) and grow with it. My management style is that of empowering people to manage their own organizations and take risks and be self-starters. I also like to interact with employees on all levels. As such, I am able to get a grassroots understanding of all employee contributions.

"I support and sponsor employee recognition, incentives, employee of the month awards, special bonuses, merit awards, and letters of commendation. I also single out employees for special training. Outside of this, I believe in verbal praise. The company backs my support. I enjoy rewarding people through recognition and having them appreciate it and seeing trusting relationships develop. It's great to be a part of a growing and intellectually stimulating environment and to flourish in this environment, plus interacting with all staff at all levels."

There are, of course, some negatives to the job. As Larry says, "Like any corporation, there is a lot of unnecessary bureaucratic red tape. I don't like it when there's a lot of politics around people's vested interests that do not have to do with the process of the project or department. We all have vested interests, but the guidelines of the department as well as the interest of the customers must come first. Some people have a vested interest in making themselves look good. They do not hire people who will challenge them, so their job is always safe. They do not give credit to people under them, giving it to themselves instead.

"Another downside is that there have been times in my career when bosses a level or two above would not let me manage. They would tell me what to do and expect me to be a robot and carry out their orders in their style. Often they were dictatorial. They would not empower me. They would not say 'I want this done . . . just do it' and let me use my style and trust it would get done."

In Larry's opinion, "Good leaders empower their people. They ask them to do things, let them go and do it their way, and ask for a report about how it is going. You need to have some boundaries and reports and weekly update meetings. There are ways of making sure it is getting done."

Advice from Larry Morin. Larry offers some very specific advice for anyone interested in a career in financial management:

"One: Learn the language and the system.

"Two: Understand what is important to you and what your values are. You'll be tested around business ethics and management. There will be times in your career that you face decisions that are not black and white, but more gray.

"Three: Make it a game and don't get too attached. Let the process develop—give logic a chance to prevail. Remember that not all decisions have to be made immediately. Live with any decision awhile. Give yourself 'time-outs' to reflect so you don't get too caught up.

"Four: Be open to luck and go with it.

"Five: Be open to relationship development, from either a potential mentor or a future student. People tend to create allegiances and teams, then mentor an individual, as the head teller did for me. It's a give-and-take relationship.

"Six: Look to the next position you want—how it will promote you and what you want from your career."

Meet Diane Camerlo, In-House Counsel, Federal Reserve Bank

Diane Camerlo works as an attorney in the legal department of the Federal Reserve Bank of St. Louis. She received her B.A. from Denison University in Granville, Ohio. In 1976, she earned her J.D. from Franklin Pierce Law Center in Concord, New Hampshire. She has been practicing law for more than twenty years.

How Diane Camerlo Got Started. "When I graduated from college with a B.A. in sociology and English, I realized my career choices were limited to low-level jobs that would only lead to careers that didn't interest me. I considered various graduate school options and chose law because I believed lawyers did interesting, challenging work and were well paid and highly respected. My father had practiced law before taking a business position, so the field was familiar to me."

In 1976 Diane began working as an associate in a law firm in Toledo, Ohio. She later became a partner in the firm, which employed about forty-five lawyers. Diane practiced mostly antitrust law, including complex litigation, and later switched to workers' compensation law.

Frustrated with compensation law, Diane left the firm and moved to Rochester, New York. She eventually began working in the corporate legal department at Monsanto, practicing antitrust and general corporate law. As an independent contractor at Monsanto, Diane did not receive paid benefits; this influenced her decision to accept a position with the Federal Reserve Bank.

As Diane describes her career thus far, "I've had experience in just about every way a lawyer can have experience except as a prosecutor, public defender, or judge."

Diane Camerlo—On the Job. The Federal Reserve Bank of St. Louis is one of the twelve operating arms of the Federal Reserve System located throughout the nation. Through its twenty-five branches, the Federal Reserve is responsible for many operations, including the administration of a nationwide payments system, distribution of the nation's currency and coin, and supervision and regulation of member banks and holding companies. The Federal Reserve also serves as banker for the U.S. Treasury.

Within this system, Diane's day typically includes meetings, client counseling, research, writing, planning, public speaking, telephone calls, traveling, and administrative duties. Diane says that on some days she might do all of these things, while on others the entire day could be devoted to any one of them. She also attends continuing education seminars and occasionally serves on business-related committees and task forces.

The attorneys in Diane's department do not practice within strict areas of specialization; instead, each works on a variety of cases. The types of law that Diane and her colleagues might practice include employment, employee benefits, contract, commercial, intellectual property, banking, general corporate, antitrust, environmental, safety, technology, tax, and litigation. The department also monitors pending federal and state legislation that affects the banking industry

Most of Diane's work involves contract, employment, banking, or technology law. She also reviews applications from bank holding companies that must be filed with the Federal Reserve. Diane says that it is common for her to be involved in twenty or more projects simultaneously. She typically works nine- to ten-hour days, but some days are even longer.

Diane describes some of the positive aspects of her job: "The atmosphere in my law department is businesslike and friendly. The lawyers usually work on individual projects, but we frequently confer with each other. This give and take among attorneys enables us to provide better legal advice to our clients and also makes the job more rewarding.

"I like the intellectual challenge and stimulation of practicing law. I like working in a corporation where I can understand the business in depth and work with the businesspeople to achieve the corporation's goals. I also enjoy the supportive atmosphere in our legal department."

A difficult aspect of the legal world is the demands it places on an attorney. As Diane says, "The primary downside to practicing law is the high level of pressure. Lawyers must give accurate legal advice, often with very short time limits. Another downside is the confrontational nature of the legal practice. Fortunately, this is much less a factor in an in-house corporate practice than in a law firm. Finally, the low opinion of lawyers held by the general public is sometimes hard to take. While there are some bad apples in the legal profession, as in all professions, in my law department we place a high value on ethical behavior and client service."

Advice from Diane Camerlo. Here is Diane's advice for those interested in a legal career: "For anyone considering a career in law, I would recommend going to the best law school possible and getting the highest grades possible. Grades are especially important. The market for new lawyers is tight, and those with low grades will have more trouble getting a job than those with high grades."

CHAPTER FIVE

Marketing and Sales Managers

anagers work in every setting—public and private—and play many different roles in their efforts to further the goals of their organizations. While many of these tasks are performed for public and nonprofit organizations, this chapter takes a close-up look at managers who preside over marketing, sales, advertising, promotions, and public relations departments in the corporate world.

The major objective of any corporation is to market and sell its products or services profitably. In small firms, the owner or chief executive officer might assume all advertising, promotions, marketing, sales, and public relations responsibilities. In large firms, which may offer numerous products and services nationally or even worldwide, an executive vice president directs overall policies for these departments. Working under the executive vice president are usually the department managers, who coordinate market research, marketing strategy, advertising, promotion, pricing, product development, sales, and public relations activities.

Marketing Managers

Marketing managers develop the firm's detailed marketing strategy. With the help of subordinates, including product development and market research managers, they determine the demand for products and services offered by the firm and its competitors. In addition, they identify potential markets, such as businesses, wholesalers, retailers, government, or the general public.

Marketing managers develop pricing strategy with an eye toward maximizing the firm's share of the market and its profits while ensuring that the firm's customers are satisfied. In collaboration with sales, product development, and other managers, they monitor trends that indicate the need for new products and services and oversee product development. Marketing managers work with advertising and promotions managers to promote the firm's products and services and to attract potential users.

Sales Managers

Sales managers direct a firm's sales program. They assign sales territories, set goals, and establish training programs for the sales representatives, to whom they recommend ways to improve their sales performance. In large, multiproduct firms, they oversee regional and local sales managers and their staffs.

Sales managers maintain contact with dealers and distributors. They analyze sales statistics gathered by their staffs to determine sales potential and inventory requirements and monitor the preferences of customers. Such information is vital for developing products and maximizing profits.

Advertising Managers

Advertising staffs in corporations are overseen by advertising managers. Except in the largest firms, advertising departments are usually small and serve as the liaison between the firm and the advertising agency to which many advertising functions are contracted out. In larger firms, advertising managers assess the need for advertising and oversee in-house account, creative, and media services departments.

Witin advertising agencies, the account executive manages the account services department and maintains the accounts of clients. The creative services department develops the concepts, subject matter, and presentation of advertising. The creative director oversees the copy chief, art director, and associated staff who design or create the advertisements. The media director oversees planning groups that select the communication media—for example, radio, television, newspapers, magazines, the Internet, or outdoor signs—to disseminate the advertising to the best target markets.

Promotions Managers

Promotions managers supervise a staff of people who specialize in this field. These managers direct publicity programs that often combine advertising with purchase incentives to increase sales in a target market. In an effort to establish closer contact with purchasers—including potential dealers and distributors as well as consumers—promotional programs are designed to reach as many targets as possible.

Promotions may involve direct mail, telemarketing, television or radio advertising, catalogs, exhibits, inserts in newspapers, Internet advertisements, websites, in-store displays or product endorsements, and special events. Purchase incentives often include discounts, samples, gifts, rebates, coupons, sweepstakes, and contests.

Public Relations Managers

Public relations managers supervise public relations specialists, directing publicity programs to a targeted public. They often specialize in a specific industry, such as health care, or in a particular area, such as crisis management. Public relations managers use every available communication medium in an effort to maintain the support of the specific group upon whom their organization's success depends, such as stockholders or the general public. For example, public relations managers may need to clarify or justify the firm's point of view on health or environmental issues to community or special-interest groups.

Public relations managers also evaluate advertising and promotional programs for compatibility with public relations efforts. In effect, they serve as the eyes and ears of top management. They observe social, economic, and political trends that might ultimately affect the firm and make recommendations to enhance the firm's image based on those trends.

Public relations managers may confer with labor relations managers to produce internal company communications, such as newsletters about employee-management relations, and with financial managers to produce company reports. They assist company executives in drafting speeches, arranging interviews, and maintaining other forms of public contact; oversee company archives; and respond to information requests. In addition, some handle special events such as sponsorship of races, parties introducing new products, or other activities the firm supports in order to gain public attention through the press without advertising directly.

Managers on the Job

Advertising, marketing, promotions, public relations, and sales managers work in offices close to those of top managers. Long hours, including evenings and weekends, are common in these positions. Working under pressure is unavoidable when schedules change and problems arise, but deadlines and goals must still be met.

Substantial travel may be involved in these managerial positions. Managers are often required to attend meetings sponsored by associations or industries related to their firms' business. Sales managers travel to national, regional, and local offices and to various dealers and distributors. Advertising and promotions managers may travel to meet with clients or representatives of communications media. At times, public relations managers travel to meet with special-interest groups or government officials. Job transfers between headquarters and regional offices are common, particularly among sales managers.

Training for Managers

A wide range of educational backgrounds is suitable for entry into advertising, marketing, promotions, public relations, and sales management jobs, but many employers prefer those with experience in related occupations plus a broad liberal arts background. A bachelor's degree in sociology, psychology, literature, journalism, or philosophy, among other subjects, is acceptable. Requirements vary, however, depending upon the particular job.

For marketing, sales, and promotions management positions, some employers prefer a bachelor's or master's degree in business administration with an emphasis on marketing. Courses in business law, economics, accounting, finance, mathematics, and statistics are advantageous. In highly technical industries, such as computer and electronics manufacturing, a bachelor's degree in engineering or science, combined with a master's degree in business administration, is preferred. (See Chapter 6 for information about careers in engineering management.)

For advertising management positions, a bachelor's degree in advertising or journalism is often preferable. A course of study should include marketing, consumer behavior, market research, sales, communication methods and technology, and visual arts— for example, art history, photography, and design.

For public relations management positions, some employers prefer a bachelor's or master's degree in public relations or journalism. Courses should include advertising, business administration, public affairs, public speaking, political science, and creative and technical writing. Courses in management and completion of an internship while in school are highly recommended for management positions in all of these specialties. Familiarity with word processing and database applications is also important for many positions. The increase in marketing, product promotion, and advertising on the Internet makes computer skills vital. The ability to communicate in a foreign language may open up employment opportunities in many rapidly growing areas around the country, especially in cities with large Spanish-speaking populations.

Several marketing and related associations sponsor national or local management training programs in collaboration with colleges and universities. Course subjects include brand and product management, international marketing, sales management evaluation, telemarketing and direct sales, interactive marketing, promotion, marketing communication, market research, organizational communication, and data processing systems procedures and management. Many firms pay all or part of the cost for those employees who successfully complete courses.

Some associations offer certification programs for managers. As a sign of competence and achievement in this field, certification is particularly important in a competitive job market. For example, Sales and Marketing Executives International offers a management certification program based on education and job performance. The Public Relations Society of America offers a certification program for public relations practitioners based on years of experience and performance on an examination. Relatively few advertising, marketing, promotions, public relations, and sales managers are currently certified, but the number of managers who seek certification is expected to grow.

The Qualities You'll Need

Anyone interested in pursuing a career in advertising, marketing, promotions, public relations, and sales management will be well served by certain personal qualities. Managers should be mature, creative, highly motivated, resistant to stress, flexible, and decisive.

Oral and written communication skills are particularly important, since managers must be able to communicate persuasively with colleagues and the public. These managers also need tact, good judgment, and exceptional ability to establish and maintain effective personal relationships with supervisory and professional staff members and client firms.

Getting Ahead

Most sales and marketing management positions are filled by promoting experienced staff or related professional personnel. Many managers are former sales representatives, purchasing agents, or specialists in products, advertising, promotions, or public relations. In small firms, where the number of positions is limited, advancement to a management position usually comes slowly. In large firms, promotion may occur more quickly.

In addition to experience and ability, managers can enhance their advancement by participating in management training programs conducted by many large firms. Many companies also provide their employees with continuing education opportunities, either in-house or at local colleges and universities, and encourage employee participation in seminars and conferences, often provided by professional associations.

Because of the importance and high visibility of their jobs, advertising, marketing, promotions, public relations, and sales managers often are prime candidates for advancement to the highest ranks. Well-trained, experienced, successful managers may be promoted to higher positions in their own, or other, firms. Some become top executives. Managers with extensive experience and sufficient capital may open their own businesses.

The Road Ahead

Employment of advertising, marketing, promotions, public relations, and sales managers is expected to grow faster than the average for all occupations through 2012, spurred by intense domestic and global competition in products and services offered to consumers. However, projected employment growth varies by industry. For example, employment is projected to grow much faster than average in scientific and professional services, such as computer-systems design, as well as in advertising and related services, as businesses increasingly hire contractors for these services instead of additional full-time staff. On the other hand, little or no change in employment is expected in many manufacturing industries.

The popularity of marketing and sales manager jobs will lead to keen competition among other managers and experienced professionals. College graduates with related experience, a high level of creativity, and strong communication skills should have the best job opportunities. Employers will particularly seek candidates who have the computer skills to conduct advertising, marketing, promotions, public relations, and sales activities on the Internet.

Salaries for Sales and Marketing Managers

According to a National Association of Colleges and Employers survey, starting salaries for marketing majors graduating in 2003 averaged $34,038; starting salaries for advertising majors averaged $29,495.

Median annual earnings for managers in 2002 were $57,130 in advertising and promotions, $78,250 in marketing, $75,040 in sales, and $60,640 in public relations. Earnings ranged from less than $30,310 for the lowest 10 percent of advertising and promotions managers to more than $145,600 for the highest 10 percent of marketing and sales managers.

Median annual earnings in the industries employing the largest numbers of marketing managers in 2002 were as follows:

Computer systems design and related services	$96,440
Management of companies and enterprises	$90,750
Banking and financial enterprises	$65,960

Median annual earnings in the industries employing the largest numbers of sales managers in 2002 were as follows:

Computer systems design and related services	$102,520
Automobile dealers	$91,350
Management of companies and enterprises	$87,800
Insurance carriers	$80,540
Traveler accommodation	$44,560

Salary levels vary substantially, depending upon the level of managerial responsibility, length of service, education, firm size, location, and industry. For example, manufacturing firms usually pay these managers higher salaries than do nonmanufacturing firms. For sales managers, the size of the sales territory is another important determinant of salary. Many managers earn bonuses equal to 10 percent or more of their salaries.

What It's Really Like

Meet Chris Fuller, Senior Vice President, General Management

Chris Fuller worked his way up through the food-services industry. He held positions of responsibility at Colgate Palmolive, Pepsi Cola, and Thomas J. Lipton before retiring.

How Chris Fuller Got Started. Chris earned both a B.A. in economics and an M.B.A. from Dartmouth College in New Hampshire. His first job was with Colgate Palmolive, which sold household products. In his next position, with General Foods, Chris was manager of marketing analysis and later became a product manager.

Chris moved on to Pepsi Cola, where he was vice president of finance and president of Metrop Bottling Company, which sold Pepsi products in the United States through company-owned franchises.

At Thomas J. Lipton, Chris was senior vice president of operations and finance and later became senior vice president of general management. That job involved marketing, and he managed a group of businesses that included the food-service end of the company.

Chris describes his initial desire to work in food services: "What attracted me to this field was that it was kind of glamorous. You had a lot of advertising and promotion. Product managers made good money, the businesses were stable, and you didn't have . . . big hiring and firing problems. You could stay with a company for a long time. They had good programs and they were well respected in the business community all over the United States."

Chris Fuller—On the Job. Chris explains that in most retail food companies, food service is secondary within the organization of the firm. It is usually a small part of the company's overall business, less profitable than other concerns.

The main purpose of the food-service industry is to sell a company's products to large clients such as restaurants and cafeterias. This often involves redesigning a common product for use by a large facility. As Chris describes it, "A tea bag that you sell to a consumer is for one cup of tea. The tea bag you'd sell to a restaurant might be for a whole jug of tea."

Chris was responsible for many different businesses during his time with Lipton. His job included Good Humor ice cream, Wishbone salad dressing, dry soups, and noodle- and rice-sauce mixes. He also managed Sahadi, a business that sold fruit rolls and other ethnic products to restaurants in areas with large Middle Eastern populations.

Chris supervised a staff member who managed the day-to-day obligations of the food-service operation. Chris's responsibilities included deciding which pricing promotions and advertising were needed to sell a product. He also determined how many salespeople were needed, what type of training they should have, where they would be posted, and which accounts they would handle.

The job includes a good deal of travel and a very tight schedule. As Chris says, "Sometimes the accounts will see you when you want to see them; sometimes you have to wait and see them another day, and here you are, having traveled three hundred miles. So what are you going to do if you don't have it planned to see other accounts in that area? There's a lot of planning and time away from home. It affects family life very negatively."

As sales manager, Chris had to travel to see the sales representatives, who cannot afford to lose sales by coming to the office to report. Less travel is required of marketing managers.

Chris points out that marketing and sales are closely related, and one can definitely affect the other: "If marketing managers are not making the expected profit, they can lose their jobs. They have the same sales volume responsibility that the salespeople have because the salespeople report to them."

The marketing manager typically makes an agreement with the sales manager to sell a specified number of units of a product. If fewer units are sold, both managers are responsible, since they agreed on the required advertising and pricing.

One of the positive aspects of the job, according to Chris, is that most successful salespeople genuinely like their jobs. As he says, "You have to like it. If you don't like walking in and talking to people every day, this job isn't for you. . . . I wouldn't say that the money is terrific. It's hard work, and you're not going to end up being wealthy. But you get a good pension plan and you get bonuses. There are a lot of incentives: trips, prizes, and cash."

Advice from Chris Fuller. Chris has some specific advice for future sales managers: "The most important thing is that you have to like traveling and meeting people and talking to people every day. You have to be able to follow directions. You're going to have a regional manager or a division manager over you who will be giving you directions, and you will have to follow those directions explicitly."

Chris also recommends some personal qualities for managers: "You need to be a gregarious person, and you have to be thick-skinned and able to take criticism. You can get a lot of complaints from a customer. . . . There's constant haranguing. . . . But it's a good career. It's a stable business."

Meet Kevin Whelan, Marketing/Product Manager

Kevin Whelan has had a long, successful career in marketing. He has been with Hill-Rom, a manufacturer of items for the health-care industry, since 1995. He earned his M.B.A. in 1982 from Georgia State University in Atlanta.

How Kevin Whelan Got Started. Kevin graduated from Spring Hill College in Mobile, Alabama, with a B.A. in history. He then served as an army officer for four years, during which he specialized in logistics, the movement of supplies or materials through distribution to an end point. When he left the army, Kevin looked for a job that would provide measurable results, preferably in a free-enterprise business.

Kevin worked for American Hospital Supply as a logistics specialist for two years, and then he was asked to consider going into sales for the company. He sold hospital supplies for one year, but as he tells it, "After one year that company was reorganizing and I was part of a reduction in force. In other words, I was canned.

"I enjoyed the job, but I did it very poorly. My first foray into sales was a disaster. I never asked people to buy anything. I would call on a hospital and show them my products. I'd ask them if they liked the products, if they liked my company, and if they liked me. And they'd always answer yes, but I never asked for the order. So getting laid off was not a surprise. I was losing money for them."

Kevin did have one very positive attribute, which was that he developed strong relationships with his customers. It was through one of these customer relationships that he was recommended for a position with Kimberly-Clark. Kevin worked for that company for ten years, five in sales and then in product management.

As Kevin says, "The rest is history. I had gone through the various stepping stones in sales—I was a senior sales rep involved with training—and I was also taking some business courses at Ohio State University at night. I was being considered for promotion into sales management, which would have been the next step. We had a marketing staff that had very little sales background, very little customer understanding. The sales manager thought I might be interested in moving into marketing to bring a sales perspective to that area.

"I stayed there for another five years. I started in marketing as an assistant product manager and left as product manager."

Kevin moved on to Hill-Rom in 1995, prompted by his interest in the acute-care business and concern for a failing market in surgical products. He liked the fact that Hill-Rom was following the health-care market into long-term care and home care, a direction he did not see his previous position taking.

Kevin Whelan—On the Job. Kevin offers a description of Hill-Rom: "We manufacture, distribute, and service health-care sleeping surfaces. This is more than just hospital beds. The term *health care* includes long-term care and home care as well as hospitals. The term *sleeping surfaces* covers more than just beds. For example, there are sleeping surfaces that are used to heal skin ulcers."

Kevin also clarifies the distinction between sales and marketing. "Salespeople try to get rid of what they have. In contrast, marketers try to get what they can get rid of. This was a corrupted quote by Ted Levitt, a marketing professor at Harvard. He said it in terms of sales companies versus marketing companies. But what the marketer does is start at the beginning of the cycle and look at the customers and say, 'Gee, I wonder what they need.' Having determined what the market needs, you then take a look at your company and try to determine if this is something you can produce for the customer. Do we know how to produce it and can we make money doing it?

"At that point we start interfacing with the product development people, who in some industries might be scientists; in my industry, it's engineers. We form a team of people—myself, the vice president of marketing, marketing researchers, engineers, advertisers, a financial advisor, and eventually salespeople—who say, 'This is something our customers really want. What can we do to meet their needs?' This is the process of idea generation. The ideas might come from talking to the customers, something we saw in a magazine, or just being out in the marketplace."

The process of idea generation includes "a lot of pleading and cajoling and trying to convince others," Kevin adds. Learning what the customers need is the end-result of market research, which often includes such strategies as setting up focus groups to hear consumers talk about what they want and need.

Once the idea has been generated and the need for a product or service verified, the marketing team moves on to concept development. A description of the product is developed and given to engineers who create a prototype. In Kevin's industry, this prototype would be a bed, which is next taken to the potential user for initial testing, also called alpha testing. During this phase, the bed is sent to a few selected facilities to solicit feedback from the health-care staff.

After the product has been refined based on user input, the final test, or beta test, is performed. At this point a patient actually uses the bed for a period of time, after which the marketers return to interview the staff about the product. The beta test is what determines whether the product will be added to the company's product line.

Simultaneously with the beta testing, the marketing staff runs additional tests for safety. They also test to be sure that the product can live up to any claims that might be made as to its features and capabilities.

The next step, according to Kevin, is that "the engineers start figuring out how to mass produce it, and I figure out how we can make money on it. For that I have to look at the cost and how much people are willing to pay for it. . . . Once I have done that, I take it to the vice president of marketing for approval."

The next stage of development is promotion and planning: "Now that I have a product, I have to find a way of getting the word out. I'll make brochures and do the advertising. This is all part of my job. I also come up with ways to teach salespeople what to say about it. At the same time I'm crunching a lot of numbers, looking to see how fast the product will be made, how fast we can get out to the field, how many will be bought, and what our projection is for making money."

When a date is set for introducing the product, Kevin holds sales meetings and tells representatives how to market the product. He then monitors the product to see if it is meeting the sales projections: "If I'm not making those numbers, my boss, the vice president of marketing, wants to know why and what I'm going to do about it. If I am making the numbers or doing better, he wants to know why and why I'm not selling more. There's no winning in this business."

Kevin's job is not done yet. He follows up with customers to find out if the product is meeting their needs or if they find that it needs to be altered. He follows up with the sales staff as well, determining what else they need to sell the product. Lastly, he follows up with the engineers to learn whether the manufacturing cost can be reduced.

Kevin typically works about fifty hours a week, and about 25 percent of his time is spent traveling. The job can be stressful, but he tries to keep that from happening. As Kevin says, "I don't choose to make it a stressful job, but it could be stressful for some people, and there are stressful times. If we're introducing a product that's not going well and sales are plummeting and we can't figure out why, it can be very stressful. In a long-term sense, my job is on the line. If sales are down on any given day, then I wouldn't be fired, but if I can't meet our profit goals over a one- to two-year period, I'd be replaced."

One of the best features of the job, for Kevin, is that he gets to do a number of different things: "My job is to influence a lot of different people, and the best way to do that is talk in their language. I have to be able to talk accounting to accountants, advertising to advertisers, patient care to nurses, sales techniques to the sales staff, engineering to our engineers, business management to the vice president of my company. No two conversations are alike."

Advice from Kevin Whelan. Kevin offers some advice regarding training for marketing managers: "The best marketers have a dual background. They have been salespeople and they also have the formal education—they have an M.B.A. My preference is to get an M.B.A. the way I did. After you've been in sales for awhile, then go back and get it."

Meet Ernie Stetenfeld, Public Relations Director

Ernie Stetenfeld is vice president of public and governmental relations for AAA Wisconsin. He has been with the organization since 1987, beginning in a general capacity and working his way up to the position of public relations director. He earned his master's degree in journalism and mass communications at Drake University in Des Moines, Iowa.

How Ernie Stetenfeld Got Started. Ernie got his start through experience in the magazine field. His graduate degree in journalism and mass communications includes two specialties, news editorial and magazine journalism. His first job was as a newspaper reporter; he then started a trade journal for the multi-housing industry in Chicago.

As Ernie says, "I enjoy magazine work, and I was hired initially at AAA because of that experience. I had also done other forms of public relations and government relations in the interim as well."

Ernie Stetenfeld—On the Job. In his capacity as public relations director, Ernie Stetenfeld was responsible for five major areas: "member relations, which is mostly a complaint-solving activity; general public relations, including news bureau activity and media relations; traffic safety promotion, which has been an AAA interest from our founding in 1902; member magazine production; and government relations and lobbying."

Ernie managed a staff of three professionals—an editor, a public relations and media manager, and a member-relations manager. He also supervised three support staff people and several others who worked for the member relations manager.

Ernie describes the function of the public relations department within the organization: "Indirectly, and more generally—and probably more importantly—my department serves in a marketing support capacity. We're the people who garner the free publicity for AAA in Wisconsin.

"We serve in a media relations capacity and are out to get the good name and logo of AAA into news media across the state, a) for public information, and b) to soften the market for our marketing purposes. Our goal is to further entrench the AAA name, logo, and reputation among the general public and our member base in the state. The purpose of this is to help them to think of us in a good way when we send them some sort of marketing pitch, such as for insurance, travel agency products, or other membership products.

"We want to create an environment for AAA in the state that disposes the general public and members to think well of us in terms of reputation and, as a result of that, to be receptive to our attempts to market products and services."

A typical day for Ernie included talking with members and giving media interviews. He wrote testimony for public policy purposes, such as to influence state legislation. He might help edit a magazine article or write a short piece for the bimonthly member publication. Most of his day, however, was spent in meetings with other department heads, trying to coordinate the activities of the various departments and doing any necessary troubleshooting.

What Ernie enjoyed most about his public relations management position was the editing, based on his experience with magazines and publications. He also enjoyed giving interviews, particularly for radio.

The downside of the job for Ernie was the government relations aspect of the work. "Sometimes the intricacies of government relations are so arcane or convoluted, and that can lead to a sense of frustration. On both federal and state levels, AAA does, to some extent on selected issues, try to influence public policy, especially as it relates to motorists or other travelers."

Ernie usually worked an average of fifty-five hours a week as public relations director. He worked Monday through Friday, and six or seven weekends each year he traveled or worked at home.

Advice from Ernie Stetenfeld. Ernie advises being prepared for many different duties: "In a PR type of job, don't expect to end up just doing one thing. In most instances, you'll be called on to relate to any number of different publics and to use any number of different communications tools, so it's best to broaden your arsenal."

CHAPTER SIX

Engineering and Natural Sciences Managers

The world of science offers opportunities for born leaders with the right combination of skills. Engineering and the natural sciences are two areas in which those with technical and scientific abilities can aspire to management positions in a wide variety of settings.

Engineering and natural sciences managers plan, coordinate, and direct research, design, and production activities. They supervise staff that may include engineers, scientists, and technicians, as well as support personnel.

Engineering and natural sciences managers use advanced technical knowledge of engineering and science to oversee a variety of activities in a wide range of industries, from professional, scientific, and technical services to manufacturing, research, and development. They work in telecommunications and utilities as well as for government agencies. They determine scientific and technical goals to fulfill the requirements of their firms. These goals may include improving manufacturing processes, advancing scientific research, or developing new products. Managers make detailed plans to accomplish these goals; for example, they may develop the overall concepts of a new product or identify technical problems preventing the completion of a project.

To effectively perform their managerial duties, they also must possess knowledge of administrative procedures, such as budgeting, hiring, and staff supervision. Engineering and natural sciences managers propose budgets for projects and programs and determine staff, training, and equipment needs. They hire and assign scientists, engineers, and support personnel to carry out specific parts of each project. They also supervise the work of these employees, review their output, and establish administrative procedures and policies, such as for environmental standards.

Engineering managers supervise people who design and develop machinery, products, systems, and processes; or they direct and coordinate production, operations, quality assurance, testing, or maintenance in industrial plants. Many are plant engineers, who coordinate the design, installation, operation, and maintenance of equipment and machinery in industrial plants. Others manage research and development teams that produce new products and processes or improve existing ones.

Natural sciences managers oversee the work of life and physical scientists, including agricultural scientists, chemists, biologists, geologists, medical scientists, and physicists. These managers direct research and development projects and coordinate activities such as testing, quality control, and production. They may work on basic research projects or on commercial activities. Science managers sometimes conduct their own research in addition to managing the work of others.

Engineering and Natural Sciences Managers on the Job

Engineering and natural sciences managers spend most of their time in an office. Some managers, however, also work in laboratories, where they may operate under the same conditions as research scientists, or in industrial plants, where they may work in the same conditions as production workers.

Most managers work at least forty hours a week, but may work much longer on occasion to meet project deadlines. Some may experience considerable pressure to meet technical or scientific goals on a short deadline or within a tight budget.

Training for Engineering and Natural Sciences Managers

Strong technical knowledge is essential for engineering and natural sciences managers, who must understand and guide the work of their subordinates and explain the work in nontechnical terms to senior management and potential customers. Therefore, management positions usually require work experience and education similar to those of engineers, scientists, or mathematicians.

Many science managers begin their careers as scientists, such as chemists, biologists, geologists, or mathematicians. Most scientists or mathematicians engaged in basic research have a Ph.D.; some in applied research and other activities may have a bachelor's or master's degree.

Science managers must be specialists in the work they supervise. In addition, employers prefer managers with good communication and administrative skills. Graduate programs allow scientists to augment their undergraduate training with instruction in other fields, such as management or computer technology. Given the rapid pace of scientific developments, science managers must continuously upgrade their knowledge.

Most engineering managers begin their careers as engineers, after completing a bachelor's degree in the field. To advance to higher-level positions, engineers generally must assume management responsibility. To fill management positions, employers seek engineers who possess administrative and communications skills in addition to technical knowledge in their specialties.

Many engineers gain these skills by obtaining a master's degree in engineering management or a master's degree in business administration (M.B.A.). Employers often pay for such training. In large firms, some courses required in these degree programs may be offered on site. Engineers who prefer management in technical areas should get a master's degree in engineering management, while those interested in nontechnical management should get an M.B.A.

Training for Engineers

Before you can be considered for an engineering management position, you will need to have worked as an engineer. A bachelor's degree in engineering is required for almost all entry-level engineering jobs. College graduates with a degree in a physical science or mathematics occasionally may qualify for some engineering jobs, particularly in specialties in high demand. Most engineering degrees are granted in electrical, electronics, mechanical, or civil engineering. However, engineers trained in one branch may work in related branches. For example, many aerospace engineers have training in mechanical engineering. This flexibility allows employers to meet staffing needs in new technologies and specialties in which engineers may be in short supply. It also allows engineers to shift to fields with better employment prospects or to those that more closely match their interests.

Most engineering programs combine a concentration of study in an engineering specialty with courses in both mathematics and science. Most programs include a design course, sometimes accompanied by a computer or laboratory class or both.

In addition to the standard engineering degree, many colleges offer two- or four-year degree programs in engineering technology. These programs usually include hands-on laboratory classes that focus on current issues. The goal is to prepare students for practical design and production work, rather than for jobs that require more theoretical and scientific knowledge.

Graduates of four-year technology programs may get jobs similar to those obtained by graduates with bachelor's degrees in engineering. Engineering technology graduates, however, are not qualified to register as professional engineers under the same terms as graduates with degrees in engineering. Some employers regard technology program graduates as having skills between those of a technician and an engineer.

Graduate training is essential for engineering faculty positions and many research and development programs but is not required for the majority of entry-level engineering jobs. Many engineers obtain graduate degrees in engineering or business administration to learn new technology and broaden their education.

About 340 colleges and universities offer bachelor's degree programs in engineering that are accredited by the Accreditation Board for Engineering and Technology (ABET), and about 240 colleges offer accredited bachelor's degree programs in engineering technology. ABET accreditation is based on an examination of an engineering program's student achievement, program improvement, faculty, curricular content, facilities, and institutional commitment. Although most institutions offer programs in the major branches of engineering, only a few offer programs in the smaller specialties. Also, programs of the same title may vary in content. For example, some programs emphasize industrial practices, preparing students for a job in industry, whereas others are more theoretical and are designed to prepare students for graduate work. Therefore, students should investigate curricula and check accreditations carefully before selecting a college.

Admissions requirements for undergraduate engineering schools include a solid background in mathematics (algebra, geometry, trigonometry, and calculus) and science (biology, chemistry, and physics) and courses in English, social studies, humanities, and computer and information technology. Bachelor's degree programs in engineering typically are designed to last four years, but many students find that it takes between four and five years to complete their studies. In a typical four-year college curriculum, the first two years are spent studying mathematics, basic sciences, introductory engineering, humanities, and social sciences. In the last two years, most courses are in engineering, usually with a concentration in one branch. Some programs offer a general engineering curriculum; students then specialize in graduate school or on the job.

Registration Requirements

All fifty states and the District of Columbia require licensure for engineers who offer their services directly to the public. Engineers who are licensed are called Professional Engineers (PEs). This licensure generally requires a degree from an ABET-accredited engineering program, four years of relevant work experience, and successful completion of a state examination. Most states recognize licensure from other states provided that the manner in which the initial license was obtained meets or exceeds their licensure requirements. Many civil, electrical, mechanical, and chemical engineers are licensed PEs.

In Canada, registration as a Professional Engineer (P.Eng.) by a provincial or territorial association of professional engineers or certification as an engineering technologist (CET) is required.

The Qualities You'll Need

Engineers and natural sciences managers should be creative, inquisitive, analytical, and detail oriented. They should be able to work as part of a team and to communicate well, both orally and in writing, because they use communication skills extensively. They spend a great deal of time coordinating the activities of their unit with those of other units or organizations. They confer with higher levels of management; with financial, production, marketing, and other managers; and with contractors and equipment and materials suppliers.

Getting Ahead

It is important for managers in both engineering and the natural sciences to continue their education throughout their careers. Much of their value to their employers depends on their knowledge of the latest advances in their field.

For instance, advances in technology have significantly affected every engineering discipline. Engineers in high-technology areas, such as advanced electronics or information technology, may find that technical knowledge can become outdated rapidly. Engineers who have not kept current in the field may find themselves passed over for promotions or vulnerable to layoffs, should they occur. By keeping current in the field, engineers are able to deliver the best solutions and greatest value to their employers. It is often these high-technology areas that offer the greatest challenges, the most interesting work, and the highest salaries.

It is equally important for natural sciences managers to continue their education and stay on the cutting edge of trends and developments in the field. Recent advances in biotechnology and information technology, combined with the use of computers to analyze complex data, have made it essential for managers in the natural sciences to continually update their knowledge base. Attending conventions and conferences and keeping abreast of the literature are essential to scientists who want to keep their edge in a rapidly changing field.

Employment Figures

Engineering and natural sciences managers held about 257,000 jobs in 2002. About 26 percent worked in professional, scientific, and technical services industries, primarily for firms providing architectural, engineering, and related services; computer systems design and related services; and scientific research and development services.

Manufacturing industries employed 35 percent of engineering and natural sciences managers. Manufacturing industries with the largest employment include those producing computer and electronic equipment, machinery, transportation equipment, aerospace products and parts, and chemicals, including agricultural products and pharmaceuticals.

Other large employers in 2002 included government agencies and telecommunications and utilities companies.

The Road Ahead

Employment of engineering and natural sciences managers is expected to grow about as fast as the average through 2012, in line with projected growth in engineering and most sciences. However, many additional jobs will result from the need to replace managers who retire or move into other occupations.

Opportunities for obtaining a management position will be best for workers with advanced technical knowledge and strong communication skills. In addition, business management skills are important because engineering and natural sciences managers are involved in their firms' financial, production, and marketing activities.

Projected employment growth for engineering and natural sciences managers should be closely related to the growth of the occupations they supervise and the industries in which they are found. For example, opportunities for managers should be better in rapidly growing areas of engineering, such as electrical, computer, and biomedical engineering, than in more slowly growing areas of engineering or physical science, such as aerospace and petroleum engineering.

In addition, many employers are finding it more efficient to contract engineering and science management services to outside companies and consultants, creating good opportunities for managers in management services and management, scientific, and technical consulting firms.

Many engineers and scientists work on long-term research and development projects or in other activities that continue even during economic slowdowns. In industries such as electronics and aerospace, however, large cutbacks in defense expenditures and government research and development funds in the past, as well as the trend toward contracting out engineering work to engineering services firms, both domestic and foreign, have resulted in significant layoffs of engineers.

Earnings for Engineering and Natural Sciences Managers

Earnings for engineering and natural sciences managers vary by specialty and level of responsibility. Median annual earnings of engineering managers were $90,930 in 2002, according to the *Occupational Outlook Handbook*. The middle 50 percent earned between $72,480 and $114,050. The lowest 10 percent earned less than $57,840; the highest 10 percent earned more than $141,380. Median annual earnings in the industries employing the largest numbers of engineering managers in 2002 were as follows:

Navigational, measuring, electromedical, and control instruments manufacturing	$101,290
Management of companies and enterprises	$98,000
Aerospace product and parts manufacturing	$97,420
Federal government	$90,030
Architectural, engineering, and related services	$89,520

Median annual earnings of natural sciences managers were $82,250 in 2002. The middle 50 percent earned between $60,000 and $111,070. The lowest 10 percent earned less than $45,640, and the highest 10 percent earned more than $144,590.

Median annual earnings in the primary fields that employed the largest numbers of natural sciences managers in 2002 were as follows:

Scientific research and development services	$101,690
Federal government	$77,020

A survey of manufacturing firms, conducted by Abbot, Langer & Associates, found that engineering department managers and superintendents earned a median annual income of $89,271 in 2003, while research and development managers earned $86,412.

In addition, engineering and natural sciences managers, especially those at higher levels, often receive more benefits—such as expense accounts, stock option plans, and bonuses—than do non-managerial workers in their organizations.

What It's Really Like

Meet George Ragsdale, Vice President, Engineering

George Ragsdale is vice president of Simmons Engineering, an engineering/design firm in Atlanta, Georgia. He graduated from Cornell University in Ithaca, New York, with a B.S. in chemical engineering in 1973. In 1992 he earned a J.D. degree and in 1993 an M.B.A., both from Widener University in Wilmington, Delaware.

How George Ragsdale Got Started. George began working in the engineering field immediately after graduating from Cornell University and began to practice law as soon as he passed the Pennsylvania Bar exam in 1992.

George describes his interest in the field: "I wanted to be a chemical engineer from the time I was in the fourth grade. I always loved chemistry and math as a child and thought that the chemical engineering field would be very challenging and interesting to me."

Once George became an engineering manager, he found that he missed actually working on engineering projects. He decided to pursue his love for the law and enrolled in law school. George says, "After graduating from law school, I continued to manage an engineering department full-time and began a family law practice on a part-time basis. Then, an opportunity arose to combine both my legal training and my engineering background, and I jumped at the chance."

George Ragsdale—On the Job. George is a senior staff manager of his firm. He supervises fifteen accountants, seven human resource professionals, and a secretary. George enjoys the diversity offered by his unique position: "One of the things I really enjoy about my current role is that every day is both different and unpredictable. Every day is a mixture of reviewing project performance, reviewing client contracts, and a lot of other things. Aside from being general counsel for our firm, I also manage the accounting, finance, and human resource functions. Each of these disciplines has its own unique challenges that are collectively guaranteed to keep each day interesting."

A typical week for George consists of working ten to eleven hours for four days, and six hours on Fridays. He also takes work home nearly every weeknight. About 20 percent of George's time is spent on the telephone, usually with other attorneys. Another 40 percent of the time is spent in meetings, and the remaining 40 percent is spent doing paperwork, primarily contract reviews.

"I consider the real upside of my job to be the opportunity to continue to learn while working at something I enjoy. Because my legal training and experience were quite narrow when I began this job, there are a lot of opportunities for me to become proficient in other areas of the law and rely less on outside counsel for assistance. The downside is that I personally have a tendency to try to do it all. And, on occasion, I overcommit because I really love what I am doing—almost too much!"

Advice from George Ragsdale. George has some advice for those with professional interests similar to his own: "For anyone who has similar interest to mine—both law and engineering—I recommend some practical experience in the engineering field first. I would also advise that in whatever field you may want to practice law, firsthand experience with the operation of that field of work provides a tremendous advantage in the legal profession over others who may not have had that practical experience."

CHAPTER SEVEN

Restaurant and Hotel Managers

Everyone eats away from home now and then, whether at a fast-food chain, elegant restaurant, or school cafeteria. Most of us also stay at a hotel on occasion. While many of us probably take restaurants and hotels somewhat for granted, both require the skills of various managers to keep operations running smoothly. In fact, we can take these establishments for granted because of good managers who work hard to keep customers happy.

Positions in Restaurant Management

Restaurant and Food-Service Managers

In addition to fast-food chains, elegant restaurants, and school cafeterias, eating establishments also include employee dining rooms and food service in hospitals and nursing facilities. The food, beverages, and services offered vary depending on the setting, but the employees of these different dining facilities share many common responsibilities.

Food-service managers are responsible for the daily operations of restaurants and other establishments that prepare and serve meals and beverages to customers. Besides coordinating activities among various departments, such as kitchen, dining room, and banquet operations, food-service managers ensure that customers are satisfied with the dining experience.

In addition, they oversee the inventory and ordering of food, equipment, and supplies and arrange for the routine maintenance and upkeep of the restaurant, equipment, and facilities. Managers generally are responsible for all of the administrative and human-resource functions of running the business, including recruiting and hiring new employees and monitoring employee performance and training.

In most full-service restaurants and institutional food-service facilities, the management team consists of a general manager, one or more assistant managers, and an executive chef.

Managers interview, hire, train, and, when necessary, fire employees. Retaining good employees is a major challenge facing food-service managers. Managers recruit employees at career fairs, contact schools that offer academic programs in hospitality or culinary arts, and arrange for newspaper advertising to attract additional applicants.

Managers oversee the training of new employees and explain the establishment's policies and practices. They schedule work hours, making sure that enough workers are present to cover each shift. If employees are unable to work, managers may have to call in alternates to cover for them or fill in themselves when needed. Some managers may help with cooking, clearing tables, or other tasks when the restaurant becomes extremely busy.

Food-service managers ensure that diners are served properly and in a timely manner. They investigate and resolve customers' complaints about food quality or service. They monitor orders in the kitchen to determine where backups may occur, and they work with the chef to remedy any delays in service.

Managers direct the cleaning of the dining areas and the washing of tableware, kitchen utensils, and equipment to comply with company and government sanitation standards. Managers also monitor the actions of their employees and patrons on a continual basis to ensure the personal safety of everyone. They make sure that health and safety standards and local liquor regulations are obeyed.

In addition to their regular duties, food-service managers perform a variety of administrative assignments, such as keeping employee work records, preparing the payroll, and completing paperwork to comply with licensing laws and reporting requirements of tax, wage and hour, unemployment compensation, and social security laws. Some of this work may be delegated to an assistant manager or bookkeeper, or it may be contracted out, but most general managers retain responsibility for the accuracy of business records. Managers also maintain records of supply and equipment purchases and ensure that accounts with suppliers are paid.

Technology influences the jobs of food-service managers in many ways, enhancing efficiency and productivity. Many restaurants use computers to track orders, inventory, and the seating of patrons. Point-of-service (POS) systems allow servers to key in a customer's order, either at the table, using a hand-held device, or from a computer terminal in the dining room, and send the order to the kitchen instantaneously so preparation can begin. The same system totals and prints checks, functions as a cash register, connects to credit-card authorizers, and tracks sales. Computers also allow restaurant and food-service managers to keep track of employee schedules and paychecks more efficiently.

Managers schedule routine services or deliveries, such as linen services or the heavy cleaning of dining rooms or kitchen equipment. They also arrange for equipment maintenance and repairs and coordinate a variety of services, such as waste removal and pest control. Managers also receive deliveries and check the contents against order records. They meet with representatives from restaurant-supply companies and place orders to replenish stocks of tableware, linens, paper products, cleaning supplies, cooking utensils, and furniture and fixtures.

Managers are also responsible for the establishment's finances. They tally the cash and charge receipts received and balance them against the record of sales at the end of each day. They are responsible for depositing the day's receipts at the bank or securing them in a safe place. Finally, managers are responsible for locking up the establishment; checking that ovens, grills, and lights are off; and switching on alarm systems.

Assistant Managers

Assistant managers in full-service facilities generally oversee service in the dining rooms and banquet areas. In larger restaurants and fast-food or other food-service facilities that serve meals daily and maintain longer hours, individual assistant managers may supervise different shifts of workers. In smaller restaurants, formal titles may be less important, and one person may undertake the work of one or more food-service positions. For example, the executive chef also may be the general manager or even sometimes an owner.

Executive Chefs

In full-service restaurants and institutional facilities, the executive chef is responsible for all food-preparation activities, including running kitchen operations, planning menus, and maintaining quality standards for food service.

Executive chefs, often in conjunction with the manager, are responsible for selecting successful menu items. This task varies by establishment depending on the use of seasonal items, how frequently the restaurant changes its menu, and the introduction of daily or weekly specials. When selecting menu items, chefs take into account the likely number of customers and the past popularity of dishes. Working with the manager, they analyze the recipes of the dishes to determine food, labor, and overhead costs and to assign prices to various dishes. Menus must be developed far enough in advance that supplies can be ordered and received in time.

Executive chefs and managers estimate food needs, place orders with distributors, and schedule the delivery of fresh food and supplies. They inspect the quality of fresh meats, poultry, fish, fruits, vegetables, and baked goods to ensure that expectations are met.

Managers on the Job

Food-service managers are among the first to arrive in the morning and the last to leave at night. Long hours—twelve to fifteen per day, fifty or more per week, and sometimes seven days a week—are common. Managers of institutional food-service facilities, such as school, factory, or office cafeterias, work more regular hours because the operating hours of these establishments usually conform to the operating hours of the business or facility they serve. For many managers, hours are unpredictable. Managers also may experience the typical minor injuries of other restaurant workers, such as muscle aches, cuts, or burns. They might endure physical discomfort from moving tables or chairs to accommodate large parties, receiving and storing daily supplies from vendors, or making minor repairs to furniture or equipment.

Training for Restaurant and Food-Service Managers

Many restaurant and food-service manager positions, especially in self-service and fast-food establishments, are filled by promoting experienced food and beverage preparation and service workers. Waiters, chefs, and fast-food workers who demonstrate potential for handling increased responsibility sometimes advance to assistant manager or management-trainee jobs. Executive chefs need extensive experience working as chefs, and general managers need prior restaurant experience, usually as assistant managers.

However, most food-service management companies and national or regional restaurant chains recruit management trainees from two- and four-year college hospitality management programs. Restaurant chains prefer to hire people who have degrees in restaurant and institutional food-service management, but they often hire graduates with degrees in other fields who have demonstrated experience, interest, and aptitude.

A bachelor's degree in restaurant and food-service management provides particularly strong preparation for a career in this occupation. A number of colleges and universities offer four-year programs in restaurant and hotel management or institutional food-service management. For those not interested in pursuing a four-year degree, community and junior colleges, technical institutes, and other institutions offer programs in the field leading to an associate's degree or other formal certification.

Both two- and four-year programs provide instruction in subjects such as nutrition, sanitation, and food planning and preparation, as well as accounting, business law and management, and computer science. Some programs combine classroom and laboratory study with internships providing on-the-job experience.

In addition, many educational institutions offer culinary programs in food preparation. Such training can lead to a career as a cook or chef and provide a foundation for advancement to an executive chef position.

Most restaurant chains and food-service management companies have rigorous training programs for management positions. Through a combination of classroom and on-the-job training, trainees receive instruction and gain work experience in all aspects of the operation of a restaurant or institutional food-service facility. Areas include food preparation, nutrition, sanitation, security, company policies and procedures, personnel management, record keeping, and preparation of reports. Training on use of the restaurant's computer system is increasingly important as well. Usually, after six months or a year, trainees receive their first permanent assignment as an assistant manager.

The Qualities You'll Need

Most employers emphasize personal qualities when hiring managers. For example, self-discipline, initiative, and leadership ability are essential. Managers must be able to solve problems and concentrate on details. They need good communication skills to deal with customers and suppliers, as well as to motivate and direct their staff. A neat and clean appearance is important, because managers must convey self-confidence and show respect in dealing with the public. Food-service management can be physically demanding, so good health and stamina also are important.

Managers should be calm, flexible, and able to work through emergencies, such as a fire or flood, in order to ensure everyone's safety. They also should be able and willing to fill in for absent workers on short notice. Managers often experience the pressures of simultaneously coordinating a wide range of activities. When problems occur, it is the manager's responsibility to resolve them with minimal disruption to customers. The job can be hectic, and dealing with irate customers or uncooperative employees can be stressful.

Getting Ahead

The certified Foodservice Management Professional (FMP) designation is a measure of professional achievement for food-service managers. Although not a requirement for employment or advancement in the occupation, voluntary certification provides recognition of professional competence, particularly for managers who acquired their skills largely on the job. The National Restaurant Association Educational Foundation awards the FMP designation to managers who achieve a qualifying score on a written examination, complete a series of courses that cover a range of food-service management topics, and meet standards of work experience in the field.

Willingness to relocate often is essential for advancement to positions with greater responsibility. Managers typically advance to larger establishments or regional management positions within restaurant chains. Some eventually open their own food-service establishments.

The Road Ahead

Employment of food-service managers is expected to grow about as fast as the average for all occupations through 2012. In addition to job openings resulting from employment growth, the need to replace managers who transfer to other occupations or stop working will create many job opportunities. Applicants with a bachelor's or an associate's degree in restaurant and institutional food-service management should have the best job opportunities.

Projected employment growth varies by industry. Most new jobs will occur in full-service restaurants and limited-service eating places as the number of these establishments increases along with the population. Manager jobs in special food services, an industry that includes food-service contractors, will increase as hotels, schools, health-care facilities, and other businesses contract out their food services to firms in this industry. Food-service manager jobs still are expected to increase in hotels, schools, and health-care facilities, but growth will be slowed as contracting out becomes more common.

Job opportunities should be better for salaried managers than for self-employed managers. More new restaurants are affiliated with national chains than are independently owned and operated. As this trend continues, fewer owners will manage restaurants themselves, and more restaurant managers will be employed by larger companies to run individual establishments.

Salaries for Restaurant and Food-Service Managers

Median annual earnings of salaried food-service managers were $35,790 in 2002. The middle 50 percent earned between $27,910 and $47,120. The lowest 10 percent earned less than $21,760, and the highest 10 percent earned more than $67,490. Median annual earnings in the industries employing the largest numbers of food-service managers in 2002 were as follows:

Special food services	$40,720
Traveler accommodation	$39,210
Full-service restaurants	$37,280
Nursing-care facilities	$33,910
Limited-service eating places	$33,590
Elementary and secondary schools	$31,210

In addition to receiving typical benefits, most salaried food-service managers are provided free meals and the opportunity for additional training, depending on their length of service.

Wages of chefs, cooks, and food-preparation workers vary greatly according to the region of the country and the type of food-service establishment in which they work. Wages usually are highest in elegant restaurants and hotels, where many executive chefs are employed, and in major metropolitan areas.

Median hourly earnings of chefs and head cooks were $13.43 in 2002. The middle 50 percent earned between $9.86 and $19.03. The lowest 10 percent earned less than $7.66, and the highest 10 percent earned more than $25.86 per hour. Median hourly earnings in the industries employing the largest number of head cooks and chefs in 2002 were as follows:

Other amusement and recreation industries	$18.31
Traveler accommodation	$17.03
Special food services	$13.98
Full-service restaurants	$12.70
Limited-service eating places	$10.49

What It's Really Like

Meet Linda Dickinson, Chef and Menu Planner, Moosewood Restaurant

Moosewood Restaurant in Ithaca, New York, opened its doors in 1973 as a collectively run vegetarian dining establishment. Part of the counterculture of the time, Moosewood workers were early adherents to the now-popular philosophy that food can be both healthful and delicious. They also believed that the workplace should be a fun place to be, with all business decisions made jointly.

Moosewood is not operated along the lines of a traditional restaurant. Members of the collective rotate through the jobs necessary to make the restaurant function, such as planning menus, preparing and serving food, setting long-term goals, and washing pots. A small staff of regular employees rounds out the group.

Initially, Moosewood Restaurant was only known locally. Now, after thirty years and several highly acclaimed cookbooks written by the collective members, Moosewood's reputation for serving fine food in a friendly atmosphere has spread nationally.

Linda began working at Moosewood in 1973. She started as a waitress but soon assumed the responsibilities of chef and menu planner. She is also coauthor of five of the collective's cookbooks: *New Recipes from the Moosewood Restaurant*, *Sundays at Moosewood Restaurant*, *Moosewood Restaurant Cooks at Home*, *Moosewood Restaurant Low-Fat Favorites*, and *Moosewood Restaurant's Book of Desserts*.

Linda Dickinson—On the Job. Linda's schedule varies depending on whether she is involved in a cookbook project: "When we're not working on a cookbook, I put in twenty to thirty hours a week at the restaurant. When we are writing, I generally never work less than two shifts, or twelve to fourteen hours. A menu-planning week is closer to thirty or forty hours, depending on how busy we are."

Linda says that this kind of schedule is different from what most restaurant workers would encounter. "Most people with a cooking position in a traditional restaurant would have to put in more hours than that. That was part of the reason Moosewood was formed as a collective. We wanted to be able to have time to do other things. Our scheduling is flexible and it varies from week to week."

On days when she is a chef, Linda consults daily with the menu planner and other cooks working on the same shift. They divide the tasks to be done and then begin cooking. Linda generally cooks for three hours prior to opening, and then she plates the food for the waiters to serve to the customers.

On menu-planning days, Linda doesn't cook. In her planning, she strives for a balance of different dishes, using seasonal ingredients. She tries to accommodate different tastes and includes dishes for vegan diners. She also considers the weather in her planning; for instance, she might offer chilled soups on hot days.

Linda checks the supplies and decides what should be ordered. She also cleans up the kitchen, receives deliveries, and cleans out the refrigerators.

Linda describes some of the realities of her job: "Moosewood is not the normal cooking situation. We have much more freedom. In a big place, you might be doing line cooking, performing one particular task, and only that, over and over. There's usually a hierarchy to deal with, too.

"We have a much friendlier situation, which doesn't mean it's not a high-pressure job. When you're in the kitchen and it's very busy, you don't get break time. You have to stay until the food is ready and the people have been served. Many times you're on your feet all day. It's a high-intensity situation. You can be under a lot of pressure. You could run out of food in the middle of a shift and have to start making more. If you don't have enough ingredients for the same dish, you might have to change the menu if you run out. You could burn things, then have to start over.

"As in any profession, there can be tensions among coworkers, and then there's the heat in the kitchen to deal with. Even though we have air conditioning, it still gets very hot with the ovens going. If you're a cook, you have to expect to be hot a lot. And it's physically demanding work, lifting heavy pots."

Despite these seeming negatives, Linda likes her job. "I'm happy with the niche I've found. Cooking seems more real to me than sitting in an office doing paperwork. You're producing a product, you're doing your best to make it good, and you're serving it to people who you hope will agree with your taste. You're trying to make food that looks appealing and tastes good. It's a real activity—you're taking care of a basic need in life."

How Linda Dickinson Got Started. Linda received her bachelor's degree in German literature in 1968 from Harper College, now SUNY Binghamton, in New York. However, she found that there were no jobs available in her field.

Linda didn't set out to work in food service. After waiting tables at various places, she began as a waiter at Moosewood in 1973. The restaurant had only been open for a couple of months, and the collective members included new employees in the decision-making process.

Linda moved into the kitchen when she made a recipe suggestion. Since the members of Moosewood were more home cooks than professional chefs, the atmosphere was more relaxed than one might expect. When Linda told the group that she knew how to make curries, she was invited into the kitchen to teach the others.

As Linda says, "In the early days, everybody who knew how to do certain dishes would teach the other cooks those dishes. I would teach other people about making curries, and they would teach me their dishes. And we were all reading cookbooks and learning how to do more things on our own.

"Because our menu changes with every meal, someone has to be in charge of planning what we would have and ordering the food for us. After the first year or two it evolved that a group of menu planners was formed, and I became one of them."

Advice from Linda Dickinson. Linda has some advice for anyone interested in working as a chef. She says that since some restaurants will only hire applicants with formal training, it is a good idea to first decide what sort of cook you want to be to determine whether formal training is necessary.

Linda suggests getting as much practice as you can: "The more experience you can get on your own—cooking at home, cooking for your friends, or observing a cook in your family—the more you can learn about cooking in general, the better it will be. But the fancier, expensive places are going to want formal training.

"If there's a restaurant you like to go to, you like the food, you could talk to some of the people who work there or the owners to see what the requirements are.

"You can also take a cooking class through adult education or at a community college or with an individual who offers a course in a particular type of cooking."

Positions in Hotel Management

Hotels and other accommodations are as diverse as the many families and business travelers they accommodate. The industry includes all types of lodging, from upscale hotels to RV parks. Motels, resorts, casino hotels, bed-and-breakfast inns, and boarding houses also are included. In fact, nearly sixty-one thousand establishments provided overnight accommodations to suit many different needs and budgets in 2002.

Hotel managers are responsible for the efficient and profitable operation of their establishments. In a small hotel, motel, or establishment with a limited staff, a single manager may direct all aspects of operations. On the other hand, large hotels may employ hundreds of workers, and the staff may include a number of assistant managers who oversee the departments responsible for various aspects of operations.

General Managers

General managers have overall responsibility for the operation of a hotel. Within guidelines established by the owners of the hotel or executives of the hotel chain, the general manager sets room rates, allocates funds to departments, approves expenditures, and establishes expected standards for guest service, decor, housekeeping, food quality, and banquet operations. Managers who work for chains also may organize and staff a newly built hotel, refurbish an older hotel, or reorganize a hotel or motel that is not operating successfully. In order to fill entry-level service and clerical jobs in hotels, some managers attend career fairs.

Computers are used extensively by lodging managers and their assistants to keep track of guests' bills, reservations, room assignments, meetings, and special events. In addition, computers are used to order food, beverages, and supplies, as well as to prepare reports for hotel owners and top-level managers. Managers work with computer specialists to ensure that the hotel's computer system functions properly. Should the hotel's computer system fail, managers must continue to meet the needs of hotel guests and staff.

Resident Managers

Resident managers live in hotels and are on call twenty-four hours a day to resolve problems or handle emergencies. In general, though, they typically work an eight- to ten-hour day. As a senior staff member, the resident manager oversees the day-to-day operations of the hotel. In many hotels, the general manager also is the resident manager.

Housekeeping Managers

Executive housekeepers ensure that guest rooms, meeting and banquet rooms, and public areas are clean, orderly, and well maintained. These managers train, schedule, and supervise the work of housekeepers and inspect rooms and order cleaning supplies.

Front-Office Managers

Front-office managers coordinate reservations and room assignments, as well as train and direct the hotel's front-desk staff. They ensure that guests are treated courteously, complaints and problems are resolved, and requests for special services are carried out.

Food and Beverage Managers

Food and beverage managers are responsible for the food services of a hotel. These managers oversee the operation of hotel restaurants, cocktail lounges, banquet facilities, and room service. They supervise and schedule food and beverage preparation and service workers, as well as plan menus, estimate costs, and deal with suppliers.

Convention-Services Managers

Convention-services managers coordinate the activities of various departments in larger hotels to accommodate meetings, conventions, and special events. They meet with representatives of groups or organizations to plan the number of rooms to reserve, the desired configuration of the meeting space, and the banquet services. During the meeting or event, they resolve unexpected problems and monitor activities to ensure that hotel operations conform to the expectations of the group.

Assistant Managers

Assistant managers help oversee the day-to-day operations of the hotel. In large hotels, they may be responsible for activities such as personnel, accounting, office administration, marketing and sales, purchasing, security, maintenance, and recreational facilities, such as the pool, spa, or exercise rooms. In smaller hotels, these duties may be combined into one position.

Hotel Managers on the Job

Because hotels are open around the clock, night and weekend work is common. Many lodging managers work more than forty hours per week. Resident managers who live in the hotel usually have regular work schedules, but they may be called to work at any time. Some employees of resort hotels are managers during the busy season and have other duties during the rest of the year.

Lodging managers sometimes experience the pressures of coordinating a wide range of functions. Conventions and large groups of tourists may present unusual problems. Moreover, dealing with irate guests can be stressful. The job can be particularly hectic for front-office managers during check-in and check-out time. Computer failures can further complicate an already busy time.

Employment Figures

Lodging managers held about sixty-nine thousand jobs in 2002. Self-employed managers—primarily owners of small hotels and motels—held about fifty percent of these jobs. Some managers were employed by companies that manage hotels and motels under contract.

Training for Hotel Personnel

In the past, many managers were promoted from the ranks of front-desk clerks, housekeepers, waiters, chefs, and hotel sales workers. Although some employees still advance to hotel management positions without education beyond high school, a college education is preferred. Restaurant management training or experience also provides a good background for entering hotel management because the success of a hotel's food-service and beverage operations often is important to the profitability of the entire establishment.

Hotels increasingly emphasize specialized training. Postsecondary training in hotel or restaurant management is preferred for most hotel management positions, although a college liberal arts degree may be sufficient when coupled with related hotel experience. Internships or part-time or summer work are an asset for students seeking a career in hotel management. The experience gained and the contacts made with employers can greatly benefit students after graduation. Most bachelor's degree programs include work-study opportunities.

Community colleges, junior colleges, and some universities offer associate's, bachelor's, and graduate degree programs in hotel or restaurant management. Combined with technical institutes, vocational and trade schools, and other academic institutions, more than eight hundred educational facilities have programs leading to formal recognition in hotel or restaurant management. Hotel management programs include instruction in hotel administration, accounting, economics, marketing, housekeeping, food-service management and catering, and hotel maintenance. Computer training also is an integral part of hotel management training, due to the widespread use of computers in reservations, billing, and housekeeping management.

Additionally, over 450 high schools in forty-five states offer the Lodging Management Program created by the Educational Institute of the American Hotel and Lodging Association. This two-year program, offered to high school juniors and seniors, teaches management principles and leads to professional certification as a Certified Rooms Division Specialist. Many colleges and universities grant participants credit toward a postsecondary degree in hotel management.

Graduates of hotel- or restaurant-management programs usually start as trainee assistant managers. Some large hotels sponsor specialized on-the-job management training programs that allow trainees to rotate among various departments and gain a thorough knowledge of the hotel's operation. Other hotels may help finance formal training in hotel management for outstanding employees. Newly built hotels, particularly those without established on-the-job training programs, often prefer to hire applicants who have hotel-management experience.

Getting Ahead

Large hotel and motel chains generally offer better opportunities for career growth than small, independently owned establishments. The large chains may have more extensive advancement programs, offering managers the opportunity to transfer to other hotels or motels in the chain or to the central office, but relocation every several years is often necessary for getting ahead.

Career advancement can be accelerated by the completion of certification programs offered by various associations. These programs usually require a combination of course work, examinations, and experience. Employers often pay the expenses for managers to complete such training courses.

The Qualities You'll Need

Lodging managers must be able to get along with many different people, even in stressful situations. They must be able to solve problems and concentrate on details. Initiative, self-discipline, effective communication skills, and the ability to organize and direct the work of others are also essential for managers at all levels.

The Road Ahead

Employment of lodging managers is expected to grow more slowly than the average for all occupations through 2012. Additional job openings are expected to occur as experienced managers transfer to other occupations or leave the labor force, in part because of the long hours and stressful working conditions. Job opportunities are expected to be best for persons with college degrees in hotel or restaurant management. Increasing business travel and domestic and foreign tourism will drive employment growth of lodging managers.

Managerial jobs are not expected to grow as rapidly as the hotel industry overall, however. As the industry consolidates, many chains and franchises will acquire independently owned establishments and increase the numbers of economy-class rooms to accommodate bargain-conscious guests. Economy hotels offer clean, comfortable rooms and front-desk services without costly extras, such as restaurants and room service. Because there are not as many departments in these hotels, fewer managers are needed.

Similarly, the increasing number of extended-stay hotels will temper demand for managers because, in these establishments, management is not required to be available twenty-four hours a day. In addition, front-desk clerks increasingly are assuming some responsibilities previously reserved for managers, further limiting the employment growth of managers and their assistants.

Additional demand for managers is expected in suite hotels because some guests, especially business customers, are willing to pay higher prices for rooms with kitchens and suites that provide the space needed to conduct meetings. In addition, large full-service hotels, offering restaurants, fitness centers, large meeting rooms, and play areas for children, among other amenities, will continue to provide many trainee and managerial opportunities.

Salaries for Hotel Managers

Median annual earnings of lodging managers were $33,970 in 2002. The middle 50 percent earned between $26,110 and $44,670. The lowest 10 percent earned less than $20,400, while the highest 10 percent earned more than $59,420.

Salaries of lodging managers vary greatly according to their responsibilities and the segment of the hotel industry in which they are employed, as well as the region where the hotel is located. Managers may earn bonuses of up to 25 percent of their base salary in some hotels. They also may be furnished with free lodging, meals, parking, laundry, and other services. In addition to providing typical benefits, some hotels offer profit-sharing plans and educational assistance to their employees.

What It's Really Like

Meet LeAnne Coury, Assistant Director of Sales

LeAnne Coury has been in the hotel and sales business for over twenty years. She works for the Quality Suites Hotel, a national chain. As assistant director of sales, she is responsible for her establishment's 207 suites and three meeting rooms.

How LeAnne Coury Got Started. After graduating from high school, LeAnne worked in the convention and sales department of the local chamber of commerce. She learned how the chamber booked events for the entire city, such as major conventions, and worked with booking blocks of hotel rooms across the city.

After a year with the chamber of commerce, LeAnne felt that her opportunities for advancement were too limited. The experience she gained on her first job helped her to move into hotel work, where better opportunities and higher salaries were more likely.

LeAnne's first hotel job was with the Red Lion, a chain of about seventy-five upscale hotels. She worked for six months, learning all that she could, and then applied for a position at a new hotel that was not yet open. LeAnne was hired as sales and convention manager.

She says, "That was a great job. They could seat a thousand people, and I pretty much ran all of that. I stayed there for three and a half years, but then an opportunity came up for me to go back to Red Lion as the sales and catering manager. It turned out to be a good move for me—more money, more knowledge."

LeAnne started working at the Quality Suites Hotel in Deerfield Beach, Florida, in 1990. She began as sales and catering manager and eventually advanced to assistant director of sales. LeAnne sees further promotion opportunities: "The next step up for me would be as director of sales, then I could even think about moving into a general manager position. The opportunities are there, and the company is willing to train me."

LeAnne Coury—On the Job. LeAnne describes her workday: "Every day is different, unlike some jobs where the work can get monotonous. The hotel industry isn't like that. You might come in in the morning with a plan to work on a specific task, then something comes up and you end up doing something else. The meeting planners for a large group convention might come in and want to discuss details with you, so you put your other work on hold for a while."

As assistant director of sales, LeAnne is responsible for bringing new business to the hotel. She looks for corporate customers who will want to use the hotel on a regular basis. This requires a lot of time on the telephone, checking details and following up with customers and service providers.

LeAnne enjoys the variety that her job offers. "I'm not just sitting at a desk. I walk around the hotel, double-check on my groups, make sure they're happy. As I said, every day is new because you're working with different people all the time. That's what I think makes it fun."

Everything about the job isn't fun, however. "As with any job," LeAnne says, "there are always some downsides. Sometimes you get bogged down with paperwork, but if you're an organized person, you should be able to stay on top of it. It's not too bad.

"Another thing in this business, a hotel never closes, so your hours won't always be the best. You could be working nights, weekends. However, I think once you put enough time in, you can move into some of the positions where you don't have such an uncertain schedule. With a smaller hotel, it's a little easier."

Overall, LeAnne finds that the advantages far outweigh the disadvantages. "In sales, you're working with some high-energy people in an up kind of atmosphere. We have bells on our desks, and when we book something we ring our bells."

Advice from LeAnne Coury. LeAnne's advice for anyone working in the hotel industry reflects the need for the right temperament and personal attributes to be successful. "If you're going to be in this industry, you have to be a people person and have a happy personality. You always have to be able to keep a smile on your face, and if a guest or a customer is dissatisfied, you have to be able to handle it. You don't ever want to lose business.

"You have to be a team player, too. If the restaurant gets busy, for example, I'll go over and help them out there. If someone needs help, then that's what you do. Our job descriptions aren't rigidly set. But it's fun to do something different once in a while."

LeAnne also advises that it is better to look for work in a corporately owned hotel rather than a smaller, family-owned franchise. The former offers more opportunities and usually higher salaries as well. Finally, she says starting out at the bottom should not be viewed as a negative: "A position at the front desk might not be the highest-paying job, but it's a good way to learn."

Meet Missy Soleau, Food and Beverage Manager

In just five years, Missy Soleau worked her way up from bussing tables to working as food and beverage manager at the Quality Suites Hotel. She works at the same property as LeAnne Coury, profiled in the previous interview.

How Missy Soleau Got Started. Missy received an associate's degree in business administration and travel and tourism from a small trade school. She intended to work in the travel industry, but she wanted to work directly with people, not behind a desk. Her job in a hotel restaurant satisfies both desires.

After initially working in the retail industry, Missy decided that she wanted to move into the hotel and restaurant field. She applied for a job at a hotel restaurant, was hired to bus tables, and a month later became a waiter.

The hotel where Missy worked was damaged by Hurricane Andrew, and she lost her job. She applied at Quality Suites and was hired as host. She worked closely with the food and beverage manager, helping him and learning at the same time. Missy was promoted to assistant food and beverage manager, and when the manager left, two years after she was initially hired, she was promoted to his position.

Missy Soleau—On the Job. Missy is responsible for scheduling the kitchen staff and ordering and purchasing food and other supplies. Since the hotel is a small property, her duties also include managing the banquet facilities.

Missy's workdays are always different. "No day is ever the same. I could be serving coffee in the morning, then participating in an executive meeting in the afternoon. And it could be that I'm here from 5:30 in the morning to 11:00 at night, if need be.

"I like to get here early in the morning, so if I do have a banquet or another event scheduled, I can see that everything is going as planned. The meeting might run until 5:00 P.M., then I have to clean up and get the room ready for another meeting that might start at 6:00. . . . I work six days a week, anywhere from fifty to sixty hours a week."

Missy is paid on a salary basis, with no overtime. She feels that although her salary is somewhat low, she is gaining valuable experience and can move to a larger hotel with the chain if she wants to. As Missy says, "I'm flexible and able to move anywhere. If I did go to a larger hotel, I'd probably start back as assistant manager again, but the salary would probably be more than I'm earning now."

Advice from Missy Soleau. Missy believes that a degree in hotel management is a valuable asset for anyone interested in working in this field: "I have no formal training in food and beverage, but

I would recommend that anyone wanting to go into this field should go to school and get a degree. Hands-on training is the best thing, I think, but in the long run, formal training can really make a difference.

"Be prepared to start off at a low salary. Eventually you'll be able to work your way up."

CHAPTER EIGHT

Medical and Health-Services Managers

Health care is a business, and, like every other business, it needs good management to keep it running smoothly. The occupation of medical and health-services manager encompasses all individuals who plan, direct, coordinate, and supervise the delivery of health care.

Large facilities usually have several assistant administrators to aid the top administrator and to handle daily decisions. Assistant administrators may direct activities in clinical areas such as nursing, surgery, therapy, medical records, or health information.

In smaller facilities, top administrators handle more of the details of daily operations. For example, many nursing-home administrators manage personnel, finance, facility operations, and admissions and have a larger role in resident care.

Medical and health-services managers include specialists and generalists. Specialists are in charge of specific clinical departments or services, while generalists manage or help to manage an entire facility or system. For example, the top administrator and assistant administrators are health-care generalists and set the overall direction of the facilities they manage. They are also concerned with community outreach, planning, policy making, and complying with government agencies and regulations. Their range of knowledge is necessarily broad, including developments in clinical departments as well as the business office. They often speak before civic groups, promote public participation in health programs, and coordinate the activities of their organizations with those of government or community agencies.

Clinical managers, on the other hand, have more specific responsibilities than do generalists, and they have training or experience in a specific clinical area. For example, directors of physical therapy are experienced physical therapists, and most health-information and medical-record administrators have a bachelor's degree in health information or medical-record administration. Clinical managers establish and implement policies, objectives, and procedures for their departments; evaluate personnel and work; develop reports and budgets; and coordinate activities with other managers.

In group medical practices, managers work closely with physicians. Whereas an office manager may handle business affairs in small medical groups, leaving policy decisions to the physicians themselves, larger groups usually employ a full-time administrator to help formulate business strategies and coordinate day-to-day business.

A small group of ten to fifteen physicians might employ one administrator to oversee personnel matters, billing and collection, budgeting, planning, equipment outlays, and patient flow. A large practice of forty to fifty physicians may have a chief administrator and several assistants, each responsible for several different areas.

Medical and health-services managers in managed-care settings perform functions similar to those of their counterparts in large group practices, except that they may have larger staffs to manage. In addition, they may do more work in the areas of community outreach and preventive care than do managers of group practices.

Some medical and health-services managers oversee the activities of a number of facilities in health systems. Such systems may contain both inpatient and outpatient facilities and offer a wide range of patient services.

Medical and Health-Services Managers on the Job

Most medical and health-services managers work long hours. Facilities such as nursing homes and hospitals operate around the clock, and administrators and managers may be called at all hours to deal with problems. They also may travel to attend meetings or inspect satellite facilities.

Some managers work in comfortable, private offices; others share space with other managers or staff. They may spend considerable time walking to consult with coworkers.

Employment Figures

Medical and health-services managers held about 244,000 jobs in 2002. About 37 percent worked in hospitals, and another 17 percent worked in offices of physicians or nursing-care facilities. The remainder worked mostly in home-health-care services, federal government health-care facilities, ambulatory facilities run by state and local governments, outpatient-care centers, insurance carriers, and community care facilities for the elderly.

Training for Medical and Health-Services Managers

Medical and health-services managers must be familiar with management principles and practices. A master's degree in health-services administration, long-term-care administration, health sciences, public health, public administration, or business administration is the standard credential for most generalist positions in this field. However, a bachelor's degree is adequate for some entry-level positions in smaller facilities and at the departmental level within health-care organizations. Physicians' offices and some other facilities may substitute on-the-job experience for formal education.

For clinical department heads, a degree in the appropriate field and work experience may be sufficient for entry. However, a master's degree in health-services administration or a related field may be required to advance. For example, nursing-service administrators usually are chosen from among supervisory registered nurses with administrative abilities and a graduate degree in nursing or health-services administration.

Bachelor's, master's, and doctoral degree programs in health administration are offered by colleges, universities, and schools of public health, medicine, allied health, public administration, and business administration. In 2003, sixty-seven schools offered accredited programs leading to the master's degree in health-services administration, according to the Accrediting Commission on Education for Health Services Administration.

Some graduate programs seek students with undergraduate degrees in business or health administration; however, many graduate programs prefer students with a background in liberal arts or health professions. Candidates with previous work experience in health care also may have an advantage. Competition for entry to these programs is keen, and applicants need above-average grades to gain admission.

Graduate programs usually last between two and three years. They may include up to one year of supervised administrative experience and course work in areas such as hospital organization and management, marketing, accounting and budgeting, human-resources administration, strategic planning, health economics, and health information systems. Some programs allow students to specialize in one type of facility—hospitals, nursing-care facilities, mental-health facilities, or medical groups. Other programs encourage a generalist's approach to education in health-care administration.

New graduates with master's degrees in health-services administration may start as department managers or as staff employees. The level of the starting position varies with the experience of the applicant and the size of the organization. Hospitals and other health facilities offer postgraduate residencies and fellowships, which usually are staff positions.

Graduates from master's degree programs also take jobs in large group medical practices, clinics, mental-health facilities, nursing-care corporations, and consulting firms.

Graduates with bachelor's degrees in health administration usually begin as administrative assistants or assistant department heads in larger hospitals. They also may begin as department heads or assistant administrators in small hospitals or nursing-care facilities.

All states and the District of Columbia require nursing-care administrators to have a bachelor's degree, pass a licensing examination, complete a state-approved training program, and pursue continuing education. A license is not required in other areas of medical and health-services management.

Getting Ahead

The structure and financing of health care is changing rapidly. Future medical and health-services managers must be prepared to deal with evolving integrated health-care delivery systems, technological innovations, an increasingly complex regulatory environment, restructuring of work, and an increased focus on preventive care. They will be called upon to improve efficiency in health-care facilities and the quality of the health care provided.

Increasingly, medical and health-services managers will work in organizations in which they must optimize the efficiency of a variety of interrelated services—for example, those ranging from inpatient care to outpatient follow-up care. Medical and health-services managers advance by moving into more responsible and higher-paying positions, such as assistant or associate administrator, or by moving to larger facilities.

The Qualities You'll Need

Medical and health-services managers often are responsible for millions of dollars' worth of facilities and equipment and hundreds of employees. To make effective decisions, they need to be open to different opinions, able to interpret data, and good at analyzing contradictory information. They also must understand finance and information systems.

Motivating others to implement their decisions requires strong leadership abilities. Tact, diplomacy, flexibility, and communication skills are essential because medical and health-services managers spend most of their time interacting with others.

The Road Ahead

Employment of medical and health-services managers is expected to grow faster than the average for all occupations through 2012 as the health-services industry continues to expand and diversify. Opportunities will be especially good in offices of physicians and other health practitioners, home-health-care services, and outpatient-care centers. Applicants with work experience in the health-care field and strong business and management skills should have the best opportunities.

Hospitals will continue to employ the most medical and health-services managers over the projected period. However, the number of new jobs created in hospitals is expected to increase at a slower rate than that in many other industries as hospitals focus on controlling costs and increasing the utilization of clinics and other alternative-care sites. Medical and health-services managers with experience in large facilities will enjoy the best job opportunities as hospitals become larger and more complex.

Employment will grow fastest in practitioners' offices and in home-health-care agencies. Many services previously provided in hospitals will continue to shift to these sectors, especially as medical technologies improve. Demand in medical group practice management will grow as medical group practices become larger and more complex.

Medical and health-services managers will need to deal with the pressures of cost containment and financial accountability, as well as with the increased focus on preventive care. They also will become more involved in trying to improve the health of their communities. Managers with specialized experience in a particular field, such as reimbursement, should have good opportunities.

Medical and health-services managers also will be employed by companies that provide management services to hospitals and other organizations, as well as to departments such as emergency, information management systems, managed-care contract negotiations, and physician recruiting.

Salaries for Medical and Health-Services Managers

Median annual earnings of medical and health-services managers were $61,370 in 2002. The middle 50 percent earned between $47,910 and $80,150. The lowest 10 percent earned less than $37,460, and the highest 10 percent earned more than $109,080.

Median annual earnings in the industries employing the largest numbers of medical and health-services managers in 2002 were as follows:

General medical and surgical hospitals	$65,950
Home-health-care services	$56,320
Outpatient-care centers	$55,650
Offices of physicians	$55,600
Nursing-care facilities	$55,320

Earnings of medical and health-services managers vary by type and size of the facility, as well as by level of responsibility. For example, the Medical Group Management Association reported that, in 2002, median salaries for administrators were $78,258 in practices with fewer than seven physicians; $92,727 in practices with seven to twenty-five physicians; and $125,988 in practices with more than twenty-six physicians.

According to a survey by *Modern Healthcare* magazine, median annual compensation in 2003 for managers of selected clinical departments was $71,800 in respiratory care; $79,000 in physical therapy; $84,500 in home health care; $85,100 in laboratory services; $89,100 in rehabilitation services; $89,500 in medical imaging or diagnostic radiology; and $98,400 in nursing services.

Salaries also varied according to size of facility and geographic region.

What It's Really Like

Meet Julie Benthal, Vice President, Nursing Administration

Julie Benthal has been a nurse for more than forty years. She now works as the top nursing administrator at a community hospital in Boca Raton, Florida.

How Julie Benthal Got Started. Julie's start in nursing came from a basic wish: "I just wanted to care for patients. . . . Before becoming vice president of nursing, I worked in critical care for years, taking care of very ill patients. I loved it."

Julie began gaining administrative experience while still a student nurse. She worked as a charge nurse, and through the years she advanced through the ranks to her present position.

Julie Benthal—On the Job. Julie is responsible for all nursing throughout the hospital. She attends many different meetings and serves on committees for budgeting and long-range planning. For Julie, this helps her to stay in touch with happenings at the facility. As she says, "It's a way of communicating and knowing what's going on in the hospital. For example, I meet with all the nurse managers once a month. We look at how we can ensure the best possible patient care and try to resolve any ongoing concerns."

Julie is also responsible for the nursing division's $20 million budget and serves on the advisory board for student nurses. In her words, "It's busy, but I enjoy it."

For Julie, the trends in health reform have led to some welcome change and innovation in the field. The move toward patient-centered care has resulted in hospitals reorganizing to better meet patients' needs.

As she describes it, "People are rethinking the way they work—not just in nursing, but in all the departments. It's a much more collaborative team effort."

The collaboration is one of the aspects of her job that Julie likes best. "I also find it rewarding that I get a chance to network a lot and share ideas and information. There's a lot of flexibility and a lot of challenge. It's never boring."

The only downside, for Julie, involves finances. "What I don't like is fighting for more stuff. That's a problem that comes up once a year when we're dealing with budgets."

Advice from Julie Benthal. Julie offers some sound advice for aspiring nursing directors. "Make sure you get several years of hands-on experience before you consider administration. And be prepared to get the right education and training. You'll have to have a master's degree in addition to your B.S.N."

Meet Laurie DeJong, Assistant Director, Physical Therapy

Laurie DeJong is assistant director of physical therapy at a large hospital in South Florida. She holds a bachelor's degree in physical therapy from Quinnipiac College in Hamden, Connecticut.

How Laurie DeJong Got Started. Laurie worked in a rehabilitation hospital for four years. Her job involved working with children and with adults on an outpatient basis. She later had a private practice for one year, offering home therapy and consultation in schools, before becoming staff physical therapist at a hospital.

Laurie's interest in the medical field began at an early age: "I always liked medical things. I started playing hospital when I was about two. My parents told me I couldn't be a nurse, but I could become a doctor if I wanted to. But when I was seventeen I realized how long it would take me to become a doctor. I learned about physical therapy from a guidance counselor, then realized that it would be the right career for me."

Laurie DeJong—On the Job. Laurie describes the work of a physical therapist: "We evaluate patients, looking for pain, their flexibility or range of motion, their strength, and what kind of functional activities they do or need to do. For example, if a patient is a dancer, she needs to dance; if it's a child, she needs to play, and so on. We do a complete evaluation . . . and then, depending upon the person and her needs, we would design an appropriate treatment plan."

In addition to the actual physical therapy, Laurie also teaches her patients, explaining exercises so that they can do them at home. She teaches patients how to prevent recurring injuries. When treating children, Laurie works with parents and teachers to help the children function at home and school and educates sports coaches about proper exercise as well. In addition, the hospital's physical-therapy staff offers classes in body awareness and risk management.

Laurie enjoys the variety that her job offers. "I can do a lot of different things. . . . I like working with the kids because I can see them for years. A child with developmental delays, such as cerebral palsy, for example, I'll see forever. We get to develop a rapport, spending time one-on-one with our patients. . . . I also like being able to keep up with the changes in health care, keeping myself on the cutting edge of what's happening out there."

Laurie describes the downside of the job: "The stresses are the same as for everyone else. There's not enough time to do the job you have to do. It's also a challenge with the changes that are happening in health care. Some of the changes aren't fun, and we don't like what's happening. There are now insurance companies telling us how we should treat our patients, as opposed to our dictating the kind of care our patients need."

Overall all, though, Laurie loves her work. She says, "It's a great profession to have. You can specialize in so many different areas. We all come out with a basic background, and then you can tailor your expertise to the area you prefer."

Advice from Laurie DeJong. Laurie's advice for anyone interested in physical therapy is fairly simple: "You have to really love working with people and you have to possess a great deal of patience. Change and improvement don't happen overnight. Often the person you're working with is impatient to get better, but you have to be the steadying force."

Professional Associations

The associations and organizations listed in this section can provide additional information about the various careers discussed throughout the book.

Chapter One: Examining the Options

The associations listed here offer a wide variety of information on general managers and top executives, including educational programs and job listings.

American Management Association
1601 Broadway
New York, NY 10019
www.amanet.org

Canadian Management Centre
150 York Street, Fifth Floor
Toronto, ON M5H 3S5
Canada
www.cmcamai.org

National Management Association
2210 Arbor Boulevard
Dayton, OH 45439
www.nma1.org

Chapter Two: Government Bigwigs

For information on careers in public administration, consult your elected representatives and local library. Information on state governments can be obtained from:

Council of State Governments
2760 Research Park Drive
P.O. Box 11910
Lexington, KY 40578
www.csg.org

Information on appointed officials in local government can be obtained from:

International City/County Management Association
777 North Capitol Street NE, Suite 500
Washington, DC 20002
www.icma.org

Chapter Three: Education Administrators

For information on elementary and secondary school principals, assistant principals, and central-office administrators, contact:

American Federation of School Administrators
1729 Twenty-First Street NW
Washington, DC 20009
www.admin.org

American Association of School Administrators
801 North Quincy Street, Suite 700
Arlington, VA 22203
www.aasa.org

Canadian Association of School Administrators
1123 Glenashton Drive
Oakville, ON L6H 5M1
Canada
www.casa-acas.ca

For information on school principals and assistant principals at the elementary and secondary levels, contact:

Canadian Association of Principals
300 Earl Grey Drive, Suite 220
Kanata, ON K2T 1C1
Canada
www.cdnprincipals.org

National Association of Elementary School Principals
1615 Duke Street
Alexandria, VA 22314
www.naesp.org

National Association of Secondary School Principals
1904 Association Drive
Reston, VA 20191
www.nassp.org

For information on careers in college and university administration, contact:

American Association of Collegiate Registrars and Admissions
  Officers
One Dupont Circle NW, Suite 520
Washington, DC 20036
www.aacrao.org

Canadian Association of College and University Student
  Services
4 Cataraqui Street, Suite 310
Kingston, ON K7K 1Z7
Canada
www.cacuss.ca

National Association of Student Personnel Administrators
1875 Connecticut Avenue NW, Suite 418
Washington, DC 20009
www.naspa.org

Chapter Four: Financial Managers

For information about careers in financial management, contact:

Financial Management Association International
University of South Florida
College of Business Administration
Tampa, FL 33620
www.fma.org

Financial Managers Society
100 West Monroe, Suite 810
Chicago, IL 60603
www.fmsinc.org

For information about financial management careers in banking and related financial institutions, contact:

American Bankers Association
1120 Connecticut Avenue NW
Washington, DC 20036
www.aba.com

Canadian Bankers Association
Box 348
Commerce Court Postal Station
199 Bay Street, Thirtieth Floor
Toronto, ON M5L 1G2
Canada
www.cba.ca

For information about financial management careers in credit unions, contact:

Credit Union Central of Canada
300 The East Mall, Suite 500
Toronto, ON M9B 6B7
Canada
www.cucentral.ca

Credit Union Executives Society
6410 Enterprise Lane, Suite 300
Madison, WI 53719
www.mortgagemag.com

For information about financial careers in business credit management, certification programs, and institutions offering graduate courses in credit and financial management, contact:

National Association of Credit Management
8840 Columbia 100 Parkway
Columbia, MD 21045
www.nacm.org

For information about careers and certification programs in treasury and corporate finance, contact:

Association for Financial Professionals
7315 Wisconsin Avenue
Bethesda, MD 20814
www.afponline.org

Financial Executives International
200 Campus Drive
P.O. Box 674
Florham Park, NJ 07932
www.fei.org

Treasury Management Association of Canada
8 King Street East, Suite 1010
Toronto, ON M5C 1B5
Canada
www.tmac.ca

For information about the Chartered Financial Analyst program, contact:

Chartered Financial Analyst (CFA) Institute
   (formerly Association for Investment Management and Research)
P.O. Box 3668
Charlottesville, VA 22903
www.cfainstitute.org

For information about financial management careers in the health-care industry, contact:

Healthcare Financial Management Association
2 Westbrook Corporate Center, Suite 700
Westchester, IL 60154
www.hfma.org

For information about careers with the Federal Reserve System, contact:

Board of Governors
Federal Reserve System
Twentieth Street and Constitution Avenue NW
Washington, DC 20551
www.federalreserve.gov

Chapter Five: Marketing and Sales Managers

For information about careers in sales and marketing management, contact:

American Marketing Association
311 South Wacker Drive, Suite 58
Chicago, IL 60606
www.marketingpower.com

Canadian Marketing Association
One Concorde Gate, Suite 607
Don Mills, ON M3C 3N6
Canada
www.the-cma.org

Sales and Marketing Executives International, Inc.
P.O. Box 1390
Sumas, WA 98295
www.smei.org

For information about careers in advertising management, contact:

American Advertising Federation
1101 Vermont Avenue NW, Suite 500
Washington, DC 20005
www.aaf.org

For information about careers in promotions management, contact:

Promotion Marketing Association, Inc.
275 Park Avenue South, Suite 1102
New York, NY 10010
www.pmalink.org

Information about careers in public relations management is available from:

Canadian Public Relations Society, Inc.
4195 Dundas Street West, Suite 346
Toronto, ON M8X 1Y4
Canada
www.cprs.ca

Public Relations Society of America
33 Maiden Lane, Eleventh Floor
New York, NY 10038
www.prsa.org

Chapter Six: Engineering and Natural Science Managers

High school students interesting in information on careers and education in engineering should contact the Junior Engineering Technical Society (JETS):

JETS—Guidance
1420 King Street, Suite 405
Alexandria, VA 22314
www.jets.org

For additional information about careers in engineering management, contact:

American Society for Engineering Education
1818 N Street NW, Suite 600
Washington, DC 20036
www.asee.org

Canadian Society of Professional Engineers
4950 Yonge Street, Suite 502
Toronto, ON M2N 6K1
Canada
www.cspe.ca

National Society of Professional Engineers
1420 King Street
Alexandria, VA 22314
www.nspe.org

Chapter Seven: Restaurant and Hotel Managers

Information about education and careers for restaurant and food-service managers, chefs, and servers is available from:

Canadian Restaurant and Foodservices Association
316 Bloor Street West
Toronto, ON M5S 1W5
Canada
www.crfa.ca

International Council on Hotel, Restaurant, and Institutional
   Education
2613 North Parham Road, Second Floor
Richmond, VA 23294
www.chrie.org

National Restaurant Association Educational Foundation
175 West Jackson Boulevard, Suite 1500
Chicago, IL 60604
www.nraef.org

For information on education and certification programs for
chefs, contact:

American Culinary Federation
180 Center Place Way
St. Augustine, FL 32095
www.acfchefs.org

For information on Canadian culinary careers, visit the website
of the Canadian Culinary Federation for its branch addresses:
www.ccfcc.ca.
For information on careers and education in hotel management, contact:

American Hotel and Lodging Association
1202 New York Avenue NW
Washington, DC 20005
www.ahla.com

Hotel Association of Canada
130 Albert Street, Suite 1206
Ottawa, ON K1P 5G4
Canada
www.hotelassociation.ca

Information about careers in housekeeping management is available from:

International Executive Housekeepers Association, Inc.
1001 Eastwind Drive, Suite 301
Westerville, OH 48081
www.ieha.org

Chapter Eight: Medical and Health-Services Managers

Information about education and career opportunities in health-care management is available from:

American College of Healthcare Executives
One North Franklin, Suite 1700
Chicago, IL 60606
www.ache.org

Canadian College of Health Service Executives
292 Somerset Street West
Ottawa, ON K2P 0J6
Canada
www.cchse.org

For information about educational programs in health-services administration, contact:

Association of University Programs in Health Administration
2000 North Fourteenth Street, Suite 780
Arlington, VA 22201
www.aupha.org

Commission on Accreditation of Healthcare Management
  Education
2000 Fourteenth Street North, Suite 780
Arlington, VA 22201
www.cahmeweb.org

For information about career opportunities in long-term-care
administration, contact:

American College of Health Care Administrators
300 North Lee Street, Suite 301
Alexandria, VA 22314
www.achca.org

For information about career opportunities in medical group
practices and ambulatory care management, contact:

Medical Group Management Association
104 Inverness Terrace East
Englewood, CO 80112
www.mgma.com

About the Author

A full-time writer of career books, Blythe Camenson works hard to help job seekers make educated choices. She firmly believes that with enough information, readers can find long-term, satisfying careers. Toward that end, she researches traditional as well as unusual occupations, talking to a variety of professionals about what their jobs are really like. In all of her books, she includes firsthand accounts from people who can reveal what to expect in each occupation.

Camenson was educated in Boston, earning her B.A. in English and psychology from the University of Massachusetts and her M.Ed. in counseling from Northeastern University.

In addition to *Careers for Born Leaders*, she has written more than two dozen books for McGraw-Hill.